Studies in Economic History

Series Editor

Tetsuji Okazaki, Faculty of Economics, The University of Tokyo, Bunkyo-ku, Tokyo, Japan

Aims and Scope

This series from Springer provides a platform for works in economic history that truly integrate economics and history. Books on a wide range of related topics are welcomed and encouraged, including those in macro-economic history, financial history, labor history, industrial history, agricultural history, the history of institutions and organizations, spatial economic history, law and economic history, political economic history, historical demography, and environmental history.

Economic history studies have greatly developed over the past several decades through application of economics and econometrics. Particularly in recent years, a variety of new economic theories and sophisticated econometric techniques—including game theory, spatial economics, and generalized method of moment (GMM)—have been introduced for the great benefit of economic historians and the research community.

At the same time, a good economic history study should contribute more than just an application of economics and econometrics to past data. It raises novel research questions, proposes a new view of history, and/or provides rich documentation. This series is intended to integrate data analysis, close examination of archival works, and application of theoretical frameworks to offer new insights and even provide opportunities to rethink theories.

The purview of this new Springer series is truly global, encompassing all nations and areas of the world as well as all eras from ancient times to the present. The editorial board, who are internationally renowned leaders among economic historians, carefully evaluate and judge each manuscript, referring to reports from expert reviewers. The series publishes contributions by university professors and others well established in the academic community, as well as work deemed to be of equivalent merit.

More information about this series at http://www.springer.com/series/13279

Donatella Strangio

Italy-China Trade Relations

A Historical Perspective

Springer

Donatella Strangio
Department Memotef
Faculty of Economics
Sapienza University of Rome
Rome, Italy

ISSN 2364-1797 ISSN 2364-1800 (electronic)
Studies in Economic History
ISBN 978-3-030-39083-9 ISBN 978-3-030-39084-6 (eBook)
https://doi.org/10.1007/978-3-030-39084-6

This Springer imprint is published by the registered company Springer Nature Switzerland AG
The registered company address is: Gewerbestrasse 11, 6330 Cham, Switzerland

Foreword by Eugenio Gaudio

The aim of this book by Donatella Strangio, Professor of Economic History at Sapienza University of Rome, is to provide a picture of the political and trade relations that Italy established with China, especially during the period between the second half of the nineteenth century and the rise of the Fascist Empire.

In addition to a detailed survey of the existing literature, the author employed various unusual sources, including the Diplomatic and Historical Diplomatic Archives at the Ministry of Foreign Affairs, as well as other archives such as the Bank of Italy's Historical Archive, the Central State Archive and the National Library.

The book reconstructs and studies the commercial and economic interests of two countries that today, in the current period of systemic globalization, are increasingly involved in a context in which, over the last quarter of a century, China, more than others, has experienced an improvement in the quality of life of most of its population.

The strength of this work lies in its analysis of the political and commercial relations between Italy and China and the history and historical processes that have accompanied them. Thus, just as the Industrial Revolution was not an immediate or impromptu event, but rather the product of changes in the economic system that occurred over the course of centuries, trade and political relations between countries are not the result of independent events, but rather the outcome of a series of actions and reactions over time.

Trade relations between Italy and China are continuously being strengthened, also thanks to a wide range of cultural initiatives. Among these, much progress has been made in cooperation between universities. In fact, the Italian academic system is working hard to attract and welcome more Chinese students and researchers, creating scholarships and exchange programmes to offer greater opportunities for the two cultures to come into direct contact and further strengthen their ties.

Sapienza University of Rome is also involved in various international credit mobility and various bilateral agreements.

In 1988, Sapienza University began its collaboration with the Zhongnan University of Economics and Law of Wuhan. The first framework agreement between the two universities was signed in 2016. Immediately afterwards, an agreement was arranged to establish the "Italo-Chinese Juridical Studies Center" with headquarters in Rome, a unique centre in Europe.

Zhongnan University arranged to send ca. 6500 volumes on juridical subjects for the Study Centre Library, which was officially inaugurated in 2017. Funding for the books, their intercontinental expedition, and their organization at the Sapienza library was arranged directly by the Chinese government. This is a further demonstration of how far-sighted this government has been in investing in cooperation—in the legal sector, in this case—between our two countries and our universities.

Italy is moving closer to China and the initiatives underway will seek to securely establish Italian firms on the Chinese market. This policy offers ample possibilities for successful Italian investment and far more.

In conclusion, considering the innovative analysis on historical events and commercial agreements concerning Italy and China carried out in this book, we may broadly assume that economic relations between the two countries will continue to grow closer, with plenty of space for further development and a positive influence on their future political and diplomatic relations.

November 2019

Eugenio Gaudio
Rector, Sapienza University of Rome

Foreword by Cristiano Variotti

2020 will be a particularly significant year for the development of bilateral relationships between Italy and China. The 50 years anniversary since the establishment of diplomatic relations between the two countries, which will align with the Italy-China Year of Culture and Tourism, does occur within a specifically meaningful political context. The visit of President Xi Jinping in Rome and Palermo in May 2019—just a few months after China removed the two presidential terms limit, thus enabling Xi to rule indefinitely—saw Italy become the first G7 country to officially endorse the Belt and Road Initiative (BRI) through the signing of a Memorandum of Understanding that stipulates the Italian-Chinese partnership for the Economic and Maritime Silk Road of the twenty-first century. It is precisely the BRI—which aims at redefining China's geopolitical role and shifting the global balance of power through its broad programme of infrastructural investments, as well as through the establishment of two new international financial organisms (Asian Infrastructure Investment Bank and Asian Development Bank) and through six brand new economic corridors linking Chinese supercities with the rest of the world—that defines the context for new opportunities of cooperation between China and Italy to unfold. To have bilateral economic relationships reach their full potential, it is necessary, nonetheless, to take meaningful preliminary steps. First of all, it is essential to reduce the information gap that limits Italian companies' ability to take strategic decisions and determines an extremely limited and stereotyped vision of China which is largely shared by most of Italian businesses. Contemporary Chinese economy is going through an intense transition, moving from a system based on low-cost (and low quality) manufacturing productions and exports to a modern system structured around services, innovation and internal market. Also, China cannot be considered as a single and homogeneous market, for it consists of geographical macro-areas with their own characteristics in terms of internal dynamics, preferences and tendencies. More than 130 cities have already exceeded one million inhabitants and more than half of luxury products' consumption is generated from cities that are not even included within the top-15 ranking. Undoubtedly, the most prominent markets for the future will be located in the so-called Tier 2 and Tier 3 cities. Nevertheless, the major urban conglomerates in the central-west areas of China are places that rarely have been taken into account by foreign enterprises for their expansion strategies. Another layer of complexity can be added when considering the level of penetration of digital technologies in the Chinese contemporary models of consumption and social interactions. The digital ecosystem, composed of platforms like Taobao, Douyin, Pinduoduo and many others, is as complex as it is strategic for the purpose of formulating commercial growth-aimed and market-devised actions in China. Getting to know the internal infrastructure is just as important as learning how to analyse the modern evolution of Chinese consumer: informed, always connected, continuously shifting towards customized models of purchasing, in terms of both products and services. A type of consumer who already satisfied his own prime needs and now majorly focuses on improving the quality of his own free time with experience-driven leisure contents, which translate into a major relevance of travel, entertainment and cultural products. This basic knowledge inevitably determines the ability to identify and seize opportunities, therefore setting efficient economic initiatives.

Largely underrated is the value of interpersonal relationships, which still stands as the backbone of business development in China: the *guanxi* works as a neuronal-like network of relationships where projects and interests are decided within. In terms of relationships building, Italy has been able to affirm a great deal of them, especially thanks to the work of diplomatic offices, trade commissions and leading entrepreneurs. Italian regions and local entities have also largely contributed at the deployment of bilateral relations with Chinese governmental departments of equal rank (even though their actions have been rarely agreed upon with and shaped around poor overall strategic view, frequently spurring from improvisation). Marche Region was, to give one example, particularly active in this field. After the first territorial friendship agreement signed in 1992 with Shandong Province (then renewed in 2012), Marche Region was able to secure a strong relation with Jiangsu (2009) and Hunan Province (2011). Two years later, this latter agreement evolved into a formal twinning between the two territories during the visit of Hunan's Governor, Mr. Du Jiahao, to Ancona (accompanied for the occasion by Mr. Zhan Chunxin, President and founder of Zoomlion, a leading construction machinery industrial group from Changsha that acquired the Italian Compagnia Italiana Forme Acciaio (CIFA) in 2008, in a rare case of successful M&A operation between China and Italy). The territorial agreements between Italian regions and Chinese provinces have generated many collaborative platforms that, in some cases, have been used by Italian SMEs in order to explore and move the first steps towards the Chinese market. Again, taking the successful example of Marche Region and Hunan Province into account, after completing the institutional architecture, sub-departments and organizations started working to establish operational platforms. New cooperative entities were thus formed, such as the Italy-China Technology Cooperation Center, established in 2014 within the Changsha High Tech Industrial Development Zone; the Low Carbon Technologies Research Center, in 2016, promoting the cooperation between Hunan Forestry Academy and Università Politecnica delle Marche; the Marche Region-Hunan Province

High-Level Training Program for Chinese Government Officials on Environmental Protection Management and Technologies, started in 2013, addressing a sector that is still strongly controlled by Chinese public authorities and that is consequentially in need of targeted political initiatives. Italian regions, by also involving intermediate entities (such as Chambers of Commerce and associations, universities, technology centres), managed to introduce innovative methods for approaching the issue of establishing valuable relations with partners, moving towards China as a territorial system and integrating heterogeneous relationships, encompassing culture, tourism, business and education. This kind of approach was seen as particularly favourable by local Chinese authorities and produced a great deal of positive outcomes.

It is not difficult to identify a certain amount of similarities between Italian and Chinese approach to business negotiation and social behaviour. Therefore, major obstacles to the deployment of effective business relations are not to be found in the domain of cross-culture compatibility. They shall eventually be searched for elsewhere. Italy lags behind schedule in terms of investments and trade volume with China, especially if compared with other European competitors like Germany and France. To explain this failure to thrive, comparative structural factors shall be taken into account: Italian and Chinese industrial manufacturing systems largely overlap, whereas German industry has significant factors of complementarity that determine its competitive advantage. Italian SMEs' cultural limitations and dimensional factors shall be also considered. Micro/small-sized family-owned businesses normally do not have cross-cultural readiness/flexibility and often lack the financial strength to operate the necessary investments to approach such a complex and far-stationed market.

At the same time, some of *Made in Italy*'s typical products clash with the extremely conservative system of Chinese culture. It is the case of the agri-food sector, which is perhaps the most disappointing performance of Italian exports to China and struggles to overcome the rigidity of Chinese consumers' taste in terms of food habits.

Finally, tariff barriers and non-tariff barriers shall be taken into account. In the case of NTBs, Italian businesses strongly perceive the uncertainty and the risks connected to the lack of protection of intellectual propriety rights, as well as the arbitrariness in the application of rules (countless examples can be pointed out and apply to a variety of contexts, from customs to tax regulations). All these "systematic" factors accumulate forming a mass of complexity, exacerbated by the anthropological italic ineptitude to overcome differences and individual interests in order to pursue a common goal. Even the best initiatives were often cut short by the unwillingness to put aside "parochialism" and thus serve a shared project.

Today, we find ourselves in front of a big turn of events. China moved its pawns on the global chessboard, setting up game-changing, yet still unknown scenarios. As always, entropy generates possibilities for those who have the ability to anticipate the full extent of change. For Italian companies, given the favourable political context, a decade of unprecedented possibilities lies ahead. Within the moderately prosper (*xiaokang*) China of our age, where leadership's validity depends mostly on the capacity of the CCP to turn into reality the imposing vision of the "Chinese dream" (*zhongguo meng*) and of the nation's rebirth, Italy must be much more than a touristic destination for wealthy Chinese people. It must be a strategic partner, it must promote its countless technological and productive excellences, it must constantly feed the relationships established with public Chinese institutions on every level, guarantee a certain extent of continuity, and it must favour an integrated approach involving government, universities, associations and private enterprises. Most importantly, on every vital junction of its public and private system, mistrust towards China must be fought with the weapons of knowledge and information. The great importance of the research work conducted by Donatella Strangio shall be analysed within this framework. The long-term history of trade relations between China and Italy shows how the past schemes of cooperation already contained the contemporary elements of success and failure, the simultaneous phases of openness and closure, as the two complementary natures of all things, the difficulties given by the rigidity of the Chinese political system, and at the same time, the great capacity of adaptation, the mutual interest, the importance of connections between individuals. All these elements converge in this research, and as we approach the reading, we shall remember that "by three methods we shall learn wisdom. First, by reflection, which is the noblest; second, by imitation, which is the easiest; third, by experience, which is the bitterest" (Confucius).

November 2019

Cristiano Variotti
Desk Manager of the Marche
Region in China

Representative for international
relations of the Hunan Province

Consular correspondent
in the Hunan Province

CEO Meilin Business
Consulting Co., Ltd

Contents

Chapter 1
Introduction

Abstract Political and trade relations between nations cannot be separated from the history and historical processes that have accompanied them over time in the relationship between the two countries. Thus, just as the Industrial Revolution was not an immediate or impromptu event, but rather the product of changes in the economic system occurring over the course of centuries, trade and political relations between countries are not the result of independent events, but rather the outcome of a series of actions and reactions over time. The aim of this book is to provide a picture of the political penetration and trade relations that Italy established with China, with particular reference to the period from the second half of the 19th century to the birth of the Fascist empire. As well as through a detailed survey of the existing literature, this work was achieved by making use of various unusual sources kept by the Diplomatic and Historical Diplomatic Archives of the Ministry of Foreign Affairs, supported by sources from other Archives such as the Bank of Italy's Historical Archive, the Central State Archive and the National Library. The book is divided into these chapters: Chap. 2 analyses the political and economic context in China until 16 the Belle Époque; Chap. 3 concerns China and its transformations during the great divergence; Chap. 4 is about the economic conditions and developments in Italy and its efforts to close the gap with the other European imperialist powers; Chap. 5 looks at Italy and China's trade and agreements; Chap. 6 deals with the relations between the two countries and the actions undertaken by Italy to penetrate China and to achieve equal standing with the other European powers there; Chap. 7 evolution of commercial relationship from 1970s to today and Chap. 8 draws some conclusions; in summarizing this historical period it shows how relations developed and changed from the golden age of the post-war period to the era of globalization.

Political and trade relations between nations cannot be separated from the history and historical processes that have accompanied them over time in the relationship between the two countries.

Thus, just as the Industrial Revolution was not an immediate or impromptu event, but rather the product of changes in the economic system occurring over the course of centuries, trade and political relations between countries are not the result of

D. Strangio, *Italy-China Trade Relations*, Studies in Economic History,
https://doi.org/10.1007/978-3-030-39084-6_1

independent events, but rather the outcome of a series of actions and reactions over time.

The aim of this book is to provide a picture of the political penetration and trade relations that Italy established with China, with particular reference to the period from the second half of the nineteenth century to the birth of the Fascist empire.

As well as through a detailed survey of the existing literature, this work was achieved by making use of various unusual sources kept by the Diplomatic and Historical Diplomatic Archives of the Ministry of Foreign Affairs, supported by sources from other Archives such as the Bank of Italy's Historical Archive, the National Library.

The Historical Diplomatic Archives of the Ministry of Foreign Affairs is structured in the form of inventories, largely of a diplomatic nature, while only two of them are concerned with trade.

However, the politically oriented inventories also contain documents and information relating to the commercial exchanges and developments that Italy carried out in China during the period under examined.

It was consulted six inventories, namely: Scritture M.A.E. del Regno d'Italia 1861–1887 (Ministry of Foreign Affairs Writings: Kingdom of Italy), Inventario Serie Poli. A 1888–1891 (Political Series Inventory A), Serie Politica P 1861–1916 (Political Series Inventory P), Inventario Serie Affari politici 1919–1930 (Political Affairs Series Inventory), Archivio del Commercio 1919–1923 and Archivio del Commercio 1924–1926 (Trade Archives).

The first three inventories contain information about the first diplomatic missions that the newly formed Kingdom of Italy undertook in China together with letters and correspondence concerning the delicate question of the religious missions in China, especially Christian ones. There is, however, very little information relating to the trade exchanges between the two countries, owing to a lack of institutions suitable for diplomatic representation and to the absence of any statistics-based research, which at that time was also lacking in data on the Italian economy.

Most of the information used came from the Political Affairs Series Inventory 1919–1930: it was in that period that Italy increased its presence in China, at both political and economic level, though far less so than the other European countries.

This inventory contains documents relating above all to the sale of arms, establishing national banks, possible mining authorizations, conferences, the reforms of treaties and customs tariffs that the foreign powers present in China requested in order to exploit the territory even further and to increase their influence there. At that time, China could be considered as a "semi-colony", at the mercy of other countries: European, Asian and American.

The two trade archives provided useful indications for the collection of trade data, since they hold letters, requests and information on institutions such as the Chamber of Commerce, the Italian Trade and Industry Agency and colonial houses.

The archive for the years 1924–1926 contains the entire basic regulation for the only Italian concession in China, that of Tientsin, which is important because very few people know about the existence of Italy's "settlements" scattered all over the world and established at a time when colonialism was an important issue, both for governments and for the general public.

Most of the information came from written documents, certified and sent by the official Italian diplomatic offices in China, specifically the Consulate General in Shanghai and the Legation in Peking, as well as from the answers and the requests made to them by the Italian Ministries. However, this work provides a general overview of Italy's past political and commercial presence in China, since it was extremely difficult to find numbers and data on trade exchanges for analytical purposes, precisely because these data are not available.

The annals and Historical Diplomatic Archives focus far more on military events than on economic data. There is a lot more information on military aspects, heroic gestures and treason than on what was sold on the markets or on import and export levels (Boulnois 2005, p. 77).

The central focus was on the glory of sovereigns, commanders and illustrious characters rather than on the practical details of ordinary people's lives; furthermore, in many great civilizations, including China, trade and traders were often despised.

With regard to the topic of this paper, the history of the relations between Italy and China boasts a very particular starting point: it was the Venetian explorer Marco Polo who first made serious political inroads into China.

In 1271, at the age of 17, he set off for the Far East with his father, Niccolò, and his uncle, in order to find new routes, new merchandise and trade facilitations to bring back to Venice, which was besieged by competition from the other maritime republics.

Marco Polo's journey lasted over twenty years, and in this period he had the chance to visit the countries and lands of the Far East, getting as far as Peking, the seat of the Great Kahn and the centre of an enormous and fabulous empire.

The Italian traveller stayed at the court of the Great Khan for several years, during which he carried out diplomatic and administrative tasks until he decided to return to Venice in 1292.

In 1298, following the battle of Curzola, he was imprisoned by the Genoese, and it was in prison that he told his cellmate, Rustichello da Pisa, about his adventures in the Far East, who then wrote them down in French, although he also included some Italian and Venetian expressions.

Once it had been published, it was not believed to be true by his contemporaries, who actually emphasized its fable-like qualities, and especially remembered the fantastic, legendary and mysterious parts.

Although even today his book "The Travels of Marco Polo" is still considered more as a book of fairy tales and marvels than as a real historical document, in reality it is the first example of modern scientific prose, providing precise and detailed information about the customs, habits, geography and economy of people and lands that were completely unknown at that time.

For many centuries, Italy's venture in China was so minimal that there are very few documents and very little evidence of its presence there, also owing to the fact that the history of Italy before its unification was extremely complicated. Over the years following Marco Polo's experiences there, China too, lost its empire and found itself almost on the margins of the economic and political system.

With regard to diplomacy, in the nineteenth century the Kingdom of Sardinia and the Kingdom of Sicily were the only states with consulates on Chinese territory, in Macao and Canton, respectively.

It was only in 1866 that a Consulate General was established, although it was more for representational than operational purposes; in 1889, some offices and branches were established to guarantee a greater breadth of operations for Italy's diplomatic Consul, Cesare Nerazzini, who was commendable for having tried to push Italy towards a greater political and economic influence in Chinese territory.

However, diplomatic relations between Italy and China in the nineteenth century can be traced back to 1866, when Italy, taking advantage of China's humiliation as a result of the Opium Wars with Great Britain, used the Arminjon Treaty to obtain the benefits and privileges that China had already had to grant to the victors and subsequently to other powers.

Yet Italy did not receive the advantages it hoped for, despite the treaty being recognized as a good starting point and being looked upon favourably in Italy. As a matter of fact, from 1866 its economic interests were extremely modest, because they were mainly based on imports of silkworms (Borsa 1994, p. 240).

The level of Italian imports and exports was embarrassing to say the least when compared with that of other foreign powers; in contrast, Italy distinguished itself, just as the other foreign powers did, by being involved in the deplorable trafficking of opium and of coolies.

For the entire nineteenth-century Italy was unable to impose an autonomous policy on a par with the other foreign states present at that time in China.

At times of crisis in the east, such as the war between China and Japan in 1894 and the Boxer Rebellion, Italy limited itself to simply supporting the decisions of the other powers, so as not to spark protests from Great Britain, the leading nation in China, also with a view to avoiding any future vetoes and obstacles or any future claims on their territory.

There were only two occasions when Italy tried to manoeuvre specifically to obtain particular benefits and to safeguard its own interests.

The first was in 1884, when Francesco Crispi tried to take advantage of the Sino-French War to claim protection for the Italian religious missions in China (a means for penetrating China and gaining influence there) which, under a clause in the 1860 Convention of Peking, was exercised by France.

Yet this attempt failed, not so much because of Chinese opposition but because of the Vatican's stance, given that they had yet to recover from the capture of Rome through Porta Pia and felt more protected by the French State.

Even more humiliating was the attempt to secure the granting of San Mun Bay and the recognition of a sphere of influence in the province of Chekiang, also because of the repercussions for Italy, which as a result suffered a governmental crisis.

The time was ripe, since China had had to give up territories to the Germans, Russians and British, leading to it being carved up. However, the undertaking was prepared very badly at diplomatic level by Italy's representatives in Italy and in

China, so much so that for the first time the Chinese found the strength to say "no" to a foreign power.

Three years later, however, Italy managed to lease an area of around 0.5 km^2 in a marshy and sparsely populated area, namely, Tientsin.

This concession should have been a starting point for a commercial penetration of China, but this was not the case, since there were almost no private or public initiatives; the government did nothing about it in the first decade of the twentieth century, virtually abandoning the concession and giving it no official recognition.

Apart from Tientsin, however, there was greater interest in China in the early years of the twentieth century, perhaps because of all the talk about the Boxer Rebellion and the benefits associated with it.

In 1904, around 700 Italians and about fifteen businessmen were working in China to build roads and railways.

There were also some initiatives of a financial nature, endorsed and supported by Italian banking groups (Società Bancaria Manzi di Roma, Società Bancaria Milanese, and Banca Commerciale Italiana), with the help of the Peking Syndicate, but with limited results (Borsa 1994, p. 242).

Yet this renewed interest did not directly involve the Italian government. In 1905, after a failed attempt to stipulate a new treaty to replace that of 1866, Giolitti, the then Prime Minister, and his successors, opted to drastically reduce Italy's presence in China. Spending was cut for the War and Naval Ministries, 700 soldiers were repatriated and the garrisons in Yangtsun and Shanhaikuan were closed too. Only a few members of the military police force stayed on in Tientsin and to defend the Legation in Peking.

Italy's presence in China had always had to contend with a chronic lack of capital, with the reluctance of Italian entrepreneurs to operate in competition or to finance risky activities, and with disorganization at both diplomatic and commercial level (Francioni 2004, p. 247).

There were nine Italian trading houses in 1900 and 133 Italian residents in the open ports.

According to the official data published by the Italian government, trade with China in 1900 amounted to imports that stood at 2.91% of total Chinese imports and exports equal to 0.32% of the total. In the years that followed, exports increased by a few tenths of a percentage point, while there was a brief dip in imports.

As well as for strictly commercial reasons, the Italian government intended to voluntarily follow a defined political policy in China, in order to maintain and improve the position it deserved as a great power, but without supporting any specific territorial ambitions, to the extent that the concession of Tientsin was only supported thanks to local taxes, and therefore at no expense for the central government in Rome.

The Italian government began to show greater interest in China towards the end of Giolitti's decade in power, as part of a new policy designed to appease nationalistic petitions and requests (Borsa 1994, p. 245).

Steps were finally taken to better organize the concession of Tientsin, thanks to some ad hoc funding in accordance with the law and provided by the Cassa Depositi e Prestiti (an Italian investment bank). Thanks also to an improvement in the commercial and financial organization, the years following the First World War saw a certain amount of increase in trade: in 1922, however, Italian imports from China, though rising in absolute terms compared with previous years, still only accounted for 0.87% of the total and exports for only 0.22%. The number of residents had also increased, partly as a result of the publicity given to the Italian Concession, but the number of trading houses remained the same: there was still a significant gap between Italy and the other countries present in China, with regard to trade, political penetration and diplomatic prestige.

A new impetus was given to Italy's presence in China between the end of the 1920s and the beginning of the 1930s, thanks to the work of Galeazzo Ciano, the Fascist Foreign Minister who was the chief diplomatic representative in China during that period.

His intervention was addressed not so much towards business and the growth of commercial traffic, which was always modest, but more in the direction of military cooperation. He actually planned to establish an aeronautical school in China with Italian instructors, and warplanes, ammunition and various weapons were sold, above all to the nationalist government.

However, this period too was characterized by delays, wishful thinking and improvisation in the attempt to define a clear Italian policy with regard to China.

Even though trade between Italy and China increased compared with the nineteenth century and with the era of Giolitti, Italy's market share in this distant eastern land was infinitely smaller than that of other countries, such as Great Britain, the USA, France and Germany.

It could conclude by stating that nowadays as in the past in China, Italy is lagging behind compared with other countries, in terms of economic cooperation and of volumes of trade. This was also due to the inadequacy of a political and entrepreneurial class that, following the announcement of the "Great Leap Forward" by Deng Xiao Ping, was unable to grasp the great opportunities offered by the Chinese market, remaining locked into its short-sighted interests and maintaining its provincial workshop mentality. It also did not realize how the political and economic world was moving towards change, towards the removal of political and trade barriers and towards a globalized world, increasingly characterized by a knowledge-based economy.

In more recent years, as a result of exchange and trade agreements, it has been broadly assumed that the economic relationship between Italy and China will become increasingly closer and provide ample margins for development, which will reinforce and have a positive influence on their future political and diplomatic relations (as shown by the data and by various economic reports, such as that of the European House—Ambrosetti). The growing trade agreement is a further stimulus towards greater cooperation and partnerships, and not only in the field of business, where an important memorandum was signed by the Ministry for Foreign Affairs and the National Development and Reform Commission of the People's Republic of China on "financial cooperation to support the development of small and medium-sized enterprises (SMEs) and the setting up of a bilateral working group in this sector". There has been progress in various other fields, including that of cooperation between universities.

Some technical barriers to economic relations still need to be removed as they are slowing down development; first of all, some issues still remain open on the application of customs duties and the forms of protection for the internal market for both sides.

Furthermore, accession to the WTO has led China to standardize the rules for international business, especially legislative issues such as the protection of investments and of copyright, and more controls on counterfeiting. In short, Italy is building a closer relationship with China, and the initiatives it has undertaken aim to achieve a concrete affirmation of its firms in the Chinese market; this policy offers ample opportunities for successful Italian investments.

The book is divided into these chapters: Chap. 2 analyses the political and economic context in China until the Belle Époque; Chap. 3 concerns China and its transformations during the great divergence; Chap. 4 is about the economic conditions and developments in Italy and its efforts to close the gap with the other European imperialist powers; Chap. 5 looks at Italy and China's trade and agreements; Chap. 6 deals with the relations between the two countries and the actions undertaken by Italy to penetrate China and to achieve equal standing with the other European powers there; and Chap. 7 evolution of commercial relationship from 1970s to today and Chap. 8 draws some conclusions; in summarizing this historical period it shows how relations developed and changed from the golden age of the post-war period to the era of globalization.

Several colleagues lent themselves in giving me valuable suggestions and advice, so thanks to Francesca Fauri, Luca Mocarelli, Gian Luca Podestà, Jacob Weisdorf; Augusto Frascani for the realization of the maps; my student Dott. Daniele Sabatini; Elizabeth Mary Bevan for helping me with the translation of the manuscript.

I dedicate this book to my parents Niny and Elio.

Chapter 2
China: Politics, History and Economy

Abstract The nineteenth century was a period of increasing heteronomy. The Chinese dynasty, overwhelmed by economic difficulties and consequent uprisings, as well as by the fragmentation of powers, determined by the extension of the empire, which had caused, since about 1820, a serious deficit in the trade balance, mainly due to the opium trade. The Opium War was triggered by England's need to safeguard the balance of triangular trade between London, Canton and India. The British troops found the Manchu government completely unprepared and above all incapable of accurately assessing the political situation and the extent of the economic relations established by foreign trade in Guandong and Guangxi. In this chapter, through the analysis of the literature, we will try to understand how all these events and others have influenced the Chinese economy, politics and society in order to understand, in the continuation of this work, the influence and role of the Italy.

2.1 Political and Social Institutions and Their Administration and Government

In the year 1840, the Chinese Empire was at its greatest extent, territorially speaking, and at that time included, as well as China itself, 18 provinces, including Manchuria, Mongolia and Tibet. Korea, Laos, Cambodia, Bhutan and Nepal, were Chinese protectorates and their emperors regularly sent lavish tributes to Peking.

The Emperor, known as the Son of Heaven, was at the head of the government, although he did not exercise his power directly; he could only either approve or reject the requests of his government officials and dignitaries.

The Emperor was served by various governing bodies, such as the Nei-ko and the Chun-chi-ch'u. The Nei-ko comprised six Grand Secretaries, who carried out the functions typical of a prime minister. The Chun-chi-ch'ù dealt mainly with military affairs and over time had replaced another governing body, the I-ch'eng-ch'u, made up of the heads of various departments and which was responsible for both civilian and military matters. Alongside these more important bodies, six Ministries (Finance,

D. Strangio, *Italy-China Trade Relations*, Studies in Economic History,
https://doi.org/10.1007/978-3-030-39084-6_2

Justice, Personnel, Rites, War and Public Works[1]) were responsible for day-to-day issues. Other bodies that were part of the administration were the Tu-ch'a-yuan, which controlled the accounting systems and the work of the civil servants and the Li-fan-yuan, which managed the coordination between the imperial court and the peoples subject to Chinese rule. Peripheral government was also characterized by an extensive bureaucracy which was divided into three levels: provinces, prefectures and districts. The officials of these government bodies were the heads of administrative units and combined the roles of administrators, judges and military commanders.

The most important local body was the province, which was a self-sufficient entity and could afford to be fairly independent from the central power base. As we will see later on, it was precisely this independence and autonomy that would make the provinces pivotal in the rebellions that led to the fall of the empire. The group of government structures formed the imperial palace complex located in the centre of Peking and where access was forbidden to anyone who was not part of the government's staff.

The family was at the heart of social life in China, headed by the father who exercised full authority and decided on his children's marriages, worked to support the family and presided over the rites to honour their ancestors (Corradini 1969, 232–233). Women played no central role in the household and were little more than servants. Their futures were decided during their adolescence, when their fathers promised them in marriage, often to boys who were younger than them. As far as religion is concerned, before the Christian missionaries arrived, most Chinese people basically followed three religious doctrines: Confucianism, Taoism and Buddhism; these were mixed with popular beliefs, namely ancestor worship and the veneration of divine and mythological Chinese heroes. The main gods were heavenly ones who protected the state and guaranteed earthly justice and earthly gods who were worshipped so that the land was prosperous and fruitful. Other gods were linked to the rivers and seas. Ancestor worship was also widely practised, especially by aristocratic families, and consisted in a series of offerings so that the spirit of the deceased would protect their households. The growth of Confucianism, Taoism and Buddhism led to the building of temples, the development of rituals and the formation of a clergy. However, visits to temples and paying attention to liturgical practices remained the prerogative of a very small share of the population, especially the wealthiest classes and intellectuals.

The main source of wealth in China was agriculture, which made it possible to ensure the survival of ninety per cent of the population. Every square metre of land and all their resources were exploited as much as possible; many hydraulic works were carried out for irrigating the land, and water has always been of vital importance in China. Natural waterways and navigable canals have always been used by its central power to enable trade between the distant outposts of the country, and by the peasant

[1]The six ministries were divided into four Directorates-General headed by two vice ministers, one of Manchu and one of Chinese origin. The Ministries of Finance and Justice were different as they had one Directorate General per province.

population to transport their food products to the cities, either to sell them or deliver them as tributes.

It was precisely the continuous building of canals over the centuries that allowed public officials, with the help of the army, to control the peasant population, and by extension, agricultural production (Pellegrini 1973, 11).

From a morphological point of view, China was characterized by large mountainous areas in the north, difficult to cultivate and inhabited by nomad populations, and vast central plains, close to the waterways where most of the population lived.

There was very little in the way of livestock, so all the hard work was done by the peasants who were constantly at work and who often joined forces to do the heaviest tasks, given that it was very rare to see ploughs being pulled by oxen at that time in China. Farmers were essentially divided into three categories: the rich, who were large landowners, the well-off, who owned plots of land which were enough to guarantee their families' livelihood, and the poor, who were forced to work on the land of the richest people and whose role differed very little from that of the serfs in medieval Europe. Nevertheless, the challenging weather conditions and the backwardness in terms of livestock meant that the best investment, given China's highly pyramidal and bureaucratic structure, was not in agriculture but rather to pass the state exams to become a member of the civil service (Corradini 1969, 236).

2.2 The Role of Foreign Powers

Europe had long begun to trade with China, although all trade went through the port of Canton, the only city to which European traders had access (Corradini 1969, 237: see also Corradini 1991a).

The vastness of China's territory and its growing population made it an attractive market for the European powers to sell their products, especially for Great Britain, the great industrial power of that time.

Great Britain was the first country, in part thanks to the most famous multinational company of that time, the British East India Company,[2] to open an embassy in Peking in 1792, to try and establish new agreements and trade treaties with China;

[2]From the second half of the sixteenth century, corporations began to operate alongside regulated companies which were more complex organizations responsible for running transcontinental trade: the British East India Company was founded in 1597 for trade with the New World, and three years later, in 1600, the East Indian Company (which up until the mid-seventeenth century was more of a regulated company than a joint stock company). Adam Smith pointed out some important events in the company's history (Smith 1976, 290 et seq.). In 1658, Oliver Cromwell, leader of the Puritan Commonwealth (1649–1660) and the inspiration behind the first Navigation Act in 1651, bestowing a new statute on the Company, according to which its capital was declared to be permanent: from then on a partner could only leave by selling their shares to other partners. From 1688, its shares were quoted on the London Stock Exchange. In 1708 it merged with another, similar company set up by the British parliament in 1698, becoming the United Company of Merchants, which lasted until 1873.

up until then, trade with European countries had been monopolized by the Cohong corporation, which paid high taxes to the state to keep this advantageous status.

Following the Continental Blockade imposed by Napoleon,[3] the East India Company had specialized in trading a new commodity through the port of Canton, opium, which was imported and paid for in silver. The consumption of opium soared, especially among the Shen Shi, or scholar-officials, who represented the Chinese elite and included intellectuals as well as state officials and members of very important families. Their ideas about society were very conservative and based on Confucian principles.[4] In first place on their scale of values were studying and idleness, in second place agricultural work, followed by a military career. Typical Western activities and professions such as trading goods and business were in last place.

Paying for opium with silver triggered a freefall in the value of copper and, given that peasants were only paid in copper for their products, this caused financial and economic problems, especially in the countryside. The consumption of opium also caused hygiene and health problems as well as a general decline in people's health. It was for this reason that in 1839, the Viceroy Lin Tsé-hsu (1758–1850), energetically resisted pressure from foreign traders and definitively banned the opium trade, confiscating and destroying dozens of crates of opium in the warehouses, especially those from Britain. An affront of this kind, together with the significant financial losses was unacceptable, and so Britain declared war on China (Corradini 1969, 239). The superiority of the British army, especially in the naval field, led to a sound defeat for the Chinese army, which was forced to sign the Treaty of Nanking in 1842, the first in a series of unequal Treaties that turned China into a kind of semi-colony. The Treaty of Nanking laid the foundations for a new era in trade relations between Great Britain and China.

It also guaranteed the opening of another four ports to European trade (Fuchow, Amoy, Ningpo and Shanghai) as well as that of Canton; the island of Hong-Kong was yielded and 21 million silver dollars were paid as an indemnity and a reimbursement for Britain's war expenses. Great Britain also obtained a most favoured nation clause, according to which a power in possession of a contract was also automatically guaranteed the concessions and advantages that China granted to third countries.

The most important clause in the Treaty, however, established a customs tariff, which could not be changed and stood at five per cent of the value of the goods. A tariff that low inevitably made it difficult to protect Chinese goods and trade was all on the side of European goods, ready to be sold to the huge Chinese population with financial profits exclusively for European traders. China's biggest concessions to

[3]This blockade banned all ships flying the British flag from docking in ports in countries under French dominion. The decree was issued by Napoleon Bonaparte in Berlin on 21 November 1806; it was extended in 1807 to include the Baltic seaports and made even stricter by the Milan Decree of the same year. The objective of the ban was to hit the British economy, given that following their defeat at Trafalgar France was no longer able either to counter British naval supremacy or to invade British soil by transporting troops by sea (see Orlandi 2016).

[4]Confucius (551 B.C.—around 479 B.C.), a Chinese philosopher who founded a school of thought whose teaching was based on morality. Its fundamental concept was that the individual, by cultivating his/her character, could to bring harmony to the human race.

foreign countries occurred in the years 1880–1890, in conjunction with the weakest period of the imperial government, caught between the grip of other countries and the discontent of the Chinese population. Aside from Great Britain, the countries most interested in penetrating China for trade were France and the USA. France wanted control of the Gulf of Tonkin, a very important commercial hub for goods from the south of China.

Attempts at reconciliation made by China having failed, in 1884 France bombed the port of Fuzhou and occupied Taiwan and the Pescadores islands. In 1885, under the Treaty of Tientsin, Vietnam was allocated to France as a protectorate, together with the total opening to trade of south-west China and full involvement in the building of railways.

As far as the USA were concerned, following their victory over Spain for control of Cuba (May 1898), they had also ensured themselves control of the Philippines, a fundamental centre for the entry of American goods into the Chinese market; for this reason they constantly asked China for full freedom of trade without preferential tariffs to the benefit of other countries.

Given its strategic position between Europe and Asia, Russia was very active, and was particularly interested in the area of Manchuria. In exchange for military and financial aid in the struggle against Japan, tsarist Russia convinced China to sign the Treaty of Moscow in 1896, which would allow them to go ahead with the construction of the Trans-Manchurian railway, and give them the rights to the mines in the connected territory, tax exemptions and the creation of a military guard and of a police force that reported exclusively to the Russian government.

Germany exploited the killing of two of its diplomats in the 1880s to demand from China the loan of the port of Jiaozhou in the Shandong Province for ninety-nine years and the construction of a fortified naval fortress and the military occupation of that territory, precluding China from any political power there. Italy also tried to gain a foothold and to put itself on the same level as the other foreign powers, but as we shall see later on, they only managed to obtain a very marshy area of about forty square kilometres near Tientsin which, instead of guaranteeing profit and wealth, required considerable investment for its reclamation.

The history of China in the nineteenth century cannot disregard the events involving and the role played by the evangelizing Christian missions. In the second half of that century, hundreds of young European and American Christians arrived in China, with a mission to convert the Chinese to Christianity, despite their strong attachment to their national rites and practices concerning ancestor worship.

Missionaries began to arrive in particularly large numbers after 1860, thanks to the extraterritorial rights afforded by the treaties (Fairbanck 1988, 164). The missionaries did not only preach the "good news"; they also built schools, hospitals and pharmacies, especially in rural areas where most of the population lived, often forgotten by rulers and government officials, who confined themselves to solving problems in the cities, leaving country dwellers to their own devices.

Yet the Chinese did not look favourably on the arrival of the missionaries, as the foreign powers exploited these missions for their own interests and for trading purposes. France in particular proclaimed itself the champion and defender of Christianity. On the pretext of protecting their missionaries, the European powers asked for and obtained the opening of consulates, embassies and legations, which played an important part in paving the way for new commercial ventures.

As we will see later on, Italy would also try and exploit the Christian missionaries to take part in trade and become a key country in the new European imperialism in the Far East, on a par with Great Britain and France.

2.3 Economic and Social Changes

Defeat in the war against the British and the drawing up of unequal treaties had led to the birth of nationalistic pride all over China, as people were furious with the government for having humiliated their country in the eyes of westerners. Between 1847 and 1850 spontaneous revolutionary movements sprang up that were given responsibilities and led by Hung-Hsiu-ch'uan, who proclaimed the advent of the "Heavenly Kingdom of Transcendent Peace". The followers of this ideology were known as Taiping, and it drew inspiration from Christianity, owing its leader coming into contact with Christian missionaries at a young age. In order to achieve their objectives, they made war on government workplaces and managed to conquer most of southern China, declaring Nanking as their capital.

The Taiping proposed important innovations, such as agrarian reforms and equality of the sexes. The former, which envisaged allocating plots of land to anyone aged sixteen and over, thus bypassing the role of household heads, failed almost entirely, given that the land in question was often overrun by war, making implementation of such reforms very difficult. In the occupied territories, however, the emancipation of women was achieved: specifically, matrimonial law was reformed and polygamy and concubinage were forbidden. Despite its initial successes, the Taiping revolution ended in failure because of disagreements among its leaders (Corradini 1969, 242). Nevertheless, the defeat of the Taiping would not have been possible without the intervention of the European powers. They had initially supported the revolt because it was more inspired by Christianity than the central government, but the Taiping wanted to regain the autonomy and did not want to recognize the principles established by the Sino-European and Sino-American treaties concluded in previous years. This annoyed the Western powers which, in exchange for helping the central government, asked for a new trade treaty.

As a result, the Treaty of Tientsin was concluded in 1861. As well as the payment of indemnities, a review of customs tariffs in favour of the Europeans and the assignment of the Chinese customs offices to Western consortia, the treaty provided for the setting up of "trade islands" by means of actual concessions on Chinese territory for France, Great Britain and the USA.

In 1864, the European army, which also included Chinese mercenaries and was known as the "always victorious Army", reconquered Nanking and thousands of Taiping soldiers were executed. Other minor revolts, such as that of the Nien-fei in the northern areas, together with famines and natural disasters devastated China in subsequent years. The destruction caused by the civil war, the misery of the military campaigns and the humiliation at international level all meant that this period was remembered by the Chinese as one of the most embarrassing in its entire history.

The situation in China following the defeat of the Taiping was disastrous to say the least. The imperial court was also beginning to recognize the need to modernize the administrative structure and the country's government, which could be done also by exploiting the technological and scientific discoveries arriving from the West. The standard bearers of this modernization were Tso Tsung-tang and Chang Chih-tung, two government officials who tried to fuse together the principles of Confucian culture with the necessary Western-style reforms. Supported by a petition signed by more than 1300 intellectuals, they asked for the creation of a modern banking system, public funding for building railways, factories and industries, a parliament elected by suffrage, and open-mindedness towards Western technical and scientific knowledge. Yet their ideas were hardly put into practice at all, except by provincial governors, conscious of the importance of radical reforms. Moreover, to ensure the birth of a "new China", substantial investment and capital were required, which could only be provided by the foreign powers. The Europeans, however, together with Japan, China's oldest enemy, had other plans: they wanted to keep China as it was, namely a kind of semi-colony that provided resources and labour.

In 1894 Japan declared war against China, as it wanted to extend its authority over Korea and remove it from traditional Chinese influence. The Japanese army, better organized and more numerous, easily defeated the Chinese. The war ended with the signing of the Treaty of Shimonoseki which imposed the following conditions on China: abandoning sovereignty over Korea, ceding Taiwan, the Pescadores islands and the Liaodong peninsula, payment of a heavy war indemnity, and opening ports for Japan to build its own factories there (Bertolozzi 2006). In the meantime, the foreign powers took advantage of this to occupy and claim rights of sovereignty over Chinese territory. The defeat of Japan, their rival Asian power, following the signing of the Treaty of Shimonoseki, stirred nationalist pride throughout the country, even in the imperial court.

In 1898 the Emperor issued a series of edicts designed to change the education system, the army and the form of government, with the aim of transforming China into a European-style country. Yet once again there were no converts to these ideas, either among the provincial governors or among the people. It was actually a provincial governor, Yuan Shin-k'ai, who, together with the Dowager Empress Cixi, organized the plot that led to the Emperor being overthrown and declared as being of unsound mind. His edicts were repealed and his advisors were executed. The Chinese became increasingly vocal in their requests for the central government to come up with a plan to rid their country of the European powers that had been acting as masters for too long.

It was for this reason that the Dowager Empress supported and financed a xenophobic organization, called the "Righteous and Harmonious Fists", better known as the "Boxers". The movement comprised people of humble origins and a low level of literacy, who hated westerners above all because their arrival had coincided with the spread of steam engines which had taken away their work. They fought without firearms, preferring bows, daggers and martial arts, including a kind of British boxing (hence the name Boxer). It was a spontaneous movement, with no leader or any kind of central organization. They were convinced that there were two reasons for China's problems: (a) the main reason for its decline was that the country had moved away from its principles and traditions in favour of Western customs and practices, which the Boxers believed were totally barbarian; and (b) the second was the inability of the imperial dynasty to stand up to foreign bullying, since it was by now considered to be crumbling, and worse still it was of Manchu rather than Chinese origin.

In the last years of the nineteenth century, there was a growing intolerance of the foreign presence in China. The Boxers had also been joined by many peasants and artisans hit by the crisis and with less and less money in their pockets as they were constantly being taxed to pay war expenses and indemnities, the latter in favour of the foreign powers. Towards the end of 1899, the Boxers began to attack Christian abbeys and missions. The Europeans responded immediately, sending an expedition of 2000 men under the command of the British Admiral Sir Edward Seymour.

The Empress Cixi was beginning to lose control of the situation and she begged the Europeans not to enter Peking, thus guaranteeing the protection of the regular Chinese army. However, when its soldiers saw foreign troops in their capital, they attacked them. On 20 June a German ambassador was killed in the street and the European armies retreated to their legations close to the "Forbidden City".[5]

The Boxers attacked the foreign legations for 55 days, but hardly managed to do any damage at all because they were disorganized, poorly armed and attacked indiscriminately, falling to rifle fire and enemy bullets. The European powers also sent reinforcements from their countries amounting to 16,000 men, comprising soldiers and soldiers from eight countries (Great Britain, France, Russia, the USA, Germany, Japan, Austria-Hungary and Italy) who entered Peking on 14 August, 1900 finally liberating the legations from the Boxers' attacks (Corradini 1969, 247). The foreign powers had everything to gain from ensuring the stability of Chinese imperial power. A weak and needy interlocutor like the imperial dynasty gave them greater freedom to use blackmail to guarantee their interests and business purposes. This explains the support given by the foreign powers to the central government to suppress the Boxers, whose rebellion had caused the deaths of 30,000 Chinese Christians, including many children. The repression carried out by the Europeans was ferocious and often indiscriminate, as the entire Chinese population was considered guilty. The Russian Cossacks and the soldiers of the British army were particularly bloodthirsty and often massacred totally innocent people. There were also many cases of theft from banks and houses in villages which had nothing to do with the rebellion. In Europe the suppression of the Boxers has always been seen as a legitimate act, provoked by their attacks on the legations and the Christian missions. Such indiscriminate violence and looting as retaliation was considered as being typical post-war behaviour.

---

[5]The Forbidden City, begun in 1406 and built in 14 years on the orders of the Emperor Ming Zhu Di, is a series of imperial buildings spread out over the centre of Peking, entrance to which was forbidden to anyone not part of the imperial court.

The Boxers are still thought of national heroes today in China, as they had had the courage to attack the "foreign devils" who, with the collusion of the Christians and the missionaries, were plundering and exploiting the riches of China for their own benefit. In early October 1900, prompted by the French, talks began to establish how much China would have to pay the European powers in reparations to compensate them for the Boxer Rebellion.

The French plan, supported by the other powers too, consisted of four main points: exemplary punishments for those who had started the rebellion; a ban on arms imports from abroad; the creation of a military corps to guard foreign legations; and substantial indemnities for companies and persons considered as victims of the rebellion. While the foreign powers held these to be legitimate requests, for the Chinese the prospect of such a treaty was nothing less than a *diktat.*

China was in no position to refuse and had to accept the conditions imposed by the European delegates. Yet negotiations went on for months, with the main issue being how much the indemnity should be. After several discussions among the victorious countries, the sum of 67 million gold sovereigns was decided, a huge amount of money at that time. China was allowed to pay what it owed in instalments spread over a period of 39 years, which meant a further increase in the amount thanks to a yearly interest rate of four per cent. The Chinese suffered yet another increase because the sum was calculated in silver, not in gold. China's monetary system was based on silver, which had gradually depreciated in recent years.

The conditions were accepted by the Chinese government and included in Article 4 of the final protocol, approved and signed in Peking on 7 September 1901.

Chapter 3
China and the Great Divergence

Abstract The splitting up of the development paths of the west and the rest of the world has been defined by economic historians as "the great divergence". Pomeranz (The great divergence: China, Europe, and the making of the modern world economy. Princeton University Press, Princeton, 2000) proposes another approach also based on the studies of Bin (China transformed: Historical change and the limits of European experience. Cornell University Press, Ithaca and London, 1997) who adopts a comparative approach to try and identify the terms of the divergence between the analysed phenomena instead of always assuming one of the two terms as the norm. In this chapter, in summary, the events arising from the politics of European imperialist powers (and some particularly poorly highlighted) in China will be analysed. Rebellions had multiplied, mainly due to the growing gap between the population and the extension of arable land. Among these, we focused on: the Taiping revolt (1851–1864), the Boxer revolt and the 1911 revolution. During the nineteenth century, the interest of the Western colonial powers grew, as well as that of Russia and subsequently of Japan: some countries considered the division of China into spheres of influence an inevitable event, even if each state pursued its own ambitions for different interests.

3.1 The End of the Empire

Dating with precision the start of the "great divergence" phase is undoubtedly complicated, given the relative scarcity of reliable macroeconomic data for Western Europe and extremely incomplete data for China in the centuries before the twentieth century. Pomeranz (2000) introduced into the international debate the doubt that the difference in income between Europe and China was due to the period preceding the Industrial Revolution. He assumes that the gap emerged after the English Industrial Revolution and then expanded during the nineteenth century until 1970, when the divergence mechanism gave way to the convergence between the incomes of the two areas under study. In this sense, Pomeranz's thesis shares some insights of the Unified

D. Strangio, *Italy-China Trade Relations*, Studies in Economic History,
https://doi.org/10.1007/978-3-030-39084-6_3

Growth Theory (Galor and Weil 2000; Galor and Moav 2004; Galor 2011),[1] namely that the European economy underwent no significant growth and that there was only sporadic in some cases, until the first twenty years of the nineteenth century. The alternative thesis, more in line with the traditional hypothesis of a European advantage over China in the centuries before the Industrial Revolution, argues instead that Europe found itself with a higher per capita income than in China, regardless of the fact that the European economy was still far its the modern growth regime.

In the years spanning the end of the nineteenth century and the beginning of the twentieth century, a figure emerged who would heavily influence events in China in the years to come: Sun Yat-sen, a Cantonese doctor who had graduated in Hong Kong and who had travelled in both Europe and the USA. He was a gifted organizer and very charismatic, and he had decided to pursue the path to revolution. Sun merged various revolutionary organizations together and founded the "United League", whose platform was based on the "Three Principles of the People" (national independence, democracy and equality) which would form the foundations of the new republican State.

In the light of what has been said previously and with regard to the divergent standard of living among the different regions of the world that was being experienced globally from the nineteenth century, onwards the new China was to base its organization on a typical Western-style system with a division of its executive, legislative and judicial powers. As a cover for his arms trafficking, in 1894 Sun founded the "society for the study of agriculture" in Canton, made up of militants who, having left Hong Kong, were supposed to occupy political and military command positions, eliminate all government officials and seize power. This revolution did not succeed, however, to the point that Sun was forced to go under cover and escape to Japan (Fairbank 1988, 191). In 1897, Sun and his supporters made another attempt at insurrection which, according to his plan would lead to the occupation of southern China, followed by a final attack on the capital. Yet this also came to nothing, because the weapons that were supposed to come from Japan were never sent, and Sun was forced to escape once again. By now, however, nationalist fervour was spreading like wildfire, especially among young Chinese people living in other countries, who were scorned and humiliated on a daily basis.

Against this backdrop, there emerged the figure of an intellectual, Liang Ch'i-ch'ao, who published a series of writings in Japan that summarized Western ideas, especially those relating to political thought and the institutional framework. Liang believed in integrating individuals into a single group, not so much because he was favourable to the liberal ideas typical of Western society, but because he believed that only the undivided effort of a people could determine the wealth and splendour of a nation. His motto was:

---

[1]The Unified Growth Theory originates in from the Malthusian scheme to explain the transition towards a defined post-Malthusian phase dominated by modest income increases up to the phase of sustained growth determined by the accumulation of human capital and technology. The construction of a dynamic system capable of explaining the transition from the Malthusian phase to a sustained growth phase requires modelling the transition between the two systems. The phase of the Industrial Revolution is the link between the two systems that Unified Growth Theory considers.

"Ten thousand eyes with one sight, ten thousand hands and feet with only one mind, ten thousand ears with one hearing … then the state is established ten-thousandfold strong" (Fairbank 1988, 193). In 1903, Liang left for the USA, where he visited several big cities and was even received by President Roosevelt. Yet Liang returned to Peking disappointed by American democracy, considering it to be too inclined towards corruption, racism and imperialism. His idea of a state was closer to the collectivist society typical of Japan and Germany. In Liang's opinion, the Chinese needed a period in which to become educated in order to assimilate the idea of a new society and to become aware citizens. Liang was not, therefore, a revolutionary: his family and social life were still governed by Confucian ideals and he was against the violence and revolutionary spirit that he thought would do more harm than good to the Chinese. He also disagreed with the ideas of Sun and his followers regarding the constitutional framework, as he thought that, rather than a republic, a constitutional monarchy was the ideal type of state for the new China (Fairbank 1988, 196).

In the years following the last failed attempt at revolution, Sun recruited new activists, mainly Chinese students from various regions of the country. The new recruits were part of various clandestine revolutionary groups, often rival ones, which were then united in 1905 by Sun into a new group, the "Revolutionary Alliance", which in the following years formed the basis for the Kuomintang (National People's Party). The objective of the Revolutionary Alliance was the advent of a new China, to be achieved through a swift revolution, and Sun was critical of Liang's attitude and way of thinking, considering him to be too moderate. And yet after several attempts at insurrection, Sun's followers were beaten once again, the Revolutionary Alliance fell apart and Sun himself resigned as its leader.

In 1905, after the attacks by Sun and his proselytes had come to nothing, the Manchu court, led by the Dowager Empress Cixi, accepted the reform package that had been scornfully rejected only a few years earlier. The granting of these reforms by the rulers was the last attempt by the government to try and save itself from a situation in which they were increasingly excluded from control of China. The biggest reforms were carried out in the schools, in the army and in the administration (Schmidt-Glintzer 2002, 45). Schools were reorganized based on the Japanese model, the private academies were reformed, the anachronistic state exam system was abolished, and a Ministry of Education was established in 1902. From a military point of view, a Ministry of War was established in 1906, the army was reorganized to be like those in Europe, and the old military exams were abolished. The army was organized into six divisions (infantry, artillery, cavalry, engineers, telegraphers and signallers), and military schools were set up with German and Japanese instructors. The person responsible for all this was Yuan Shih-k'ai, the then governor of Tientsin who would become President of the Chinese Republic. The process of modernization strengthened the local provincial militias rather than the central army, which were commanded by the "warlords".

On the eve of 1910, the reforms had undoubtedly contributed to the progress of the Chinese army, although it could not yet be described as a modern army. It lacked trained officers, the Military Staff was inexperienced and the supply of munitions was inadequate. With the equipment and organization it had at that time, China could easily maintain order within its borders, but it would not have been able to resist attacks from European, American or Japanese armies.[2] As far as administration and government were concerned, imperial authority was reinforced and consent was given for the establishment of a parliament. It was only in 1909 that the first provincial assemblies began to meet, and their work helped to weaken the central government. The provincial and municipal governments created new departments for agriculture, foreign affairs, the police force, trade and industry. There was greater focus and more support for private economic enterprise, corporations similar to Western Chambers of Commerce were set up and, in 1902, the Ministry of Commerce was founded in Peking.

One of the most necessary reforms was to the tax system, as the tax burden in China was by no means excessive, but the high level of tax evasion among the rich and powerful meant that small-scale producers and peasants had to pay a great deal in taxes. It was not until 1910 that an attempt was made to set up a national budget, but the idea did not become a reality as each province acted on its own behalf, setting rates and taxes autonomously. By now, however, the Manchu dynasty in power was no longer able to obtain the consensus of the people and these reforms actually weakened the empire rather than making it stronger.

These reforms were carried out from above, the people were not consulted, and neither were peripheral governments listened to or involved in any way in the reform process. The building of schools, industries and hospitals did not lead to an overall improvement in living conditions for peasants, who actually had to pay more taxes to finance the above-mentioned reforms (Fairbank 1988, 208). The area most active in causing the crisis to gather speed and the fall of the empire was that of the provinces. A province in China covered a great deal of land (similar to the area of a European country) which guaranteed its autonomy, financial strength and political freedom. Each province had its own traditions, customs and festivities and saw the rise of a new dominant class that of the minor rural nobility, destined to be decisive in the future social and institutional framework. The growth in investment in land had increased its value exponentially, and landowners moved to the cities to manage their affairs, putting an end to the traditional relationship between landlords and their peasants, which now became a typical "employer-employee" market relationship. This new social class gradually became wealthier and its members were transformed from being well-off rural landowners into urban industrialists, who invested their savings in the land. This was similar to the situation in the USA, where the great agrarian industries in the north created competition that the farms in the south had to face and which was one of the causes of the War of Succession between the Confederate States and the Union. It was of course the Chinese peasants who paid the price for all this, and not only were they burdened with new taxes, they also saw their living conditions worsen to the point that they became the slaves of the new agrarian capitalists.

[2]Historical Diplomatic Archives of the Ministry of Foreign Affairs, Political Series P 1891–1916, Pacco 511, *Purchase and construction of warships*, The Chinese army on 1 March 1910, Bulletin No. 15 of the Italian Military Staff Corps Command, Colonial Office.

The exploitation of the peasants was also made easier by the fact that these new landowners used military force as a threat. These military forces were paid directly by the local lords and formed personal militias that were independent from the central government. This was how the "warlords" came into being, as after the Republic was proclaimed in 1911, they became the real holders of financial and political power in China.

As a result of all this, the revolution of 1911 was simply the end of an epoch and a historical era. The Qing dynasty, increasingly unpopular with its people, disappeared by itself, with no need for bloodletting or ferocious rebellions. The main event that actually led to the fall of the empire was the events on the "Double Ten" on 10 October 1911 (Schmidt-Glintzer 2002, 46). A conspiracy was uncovered in Hankou following the explosion of a bomb in the Russian Legation. More than 3000 soldiers mutinied, refusing to obey the orders of the Manchu generals and military commanders who were forced to escape, leaving the power and leadership of the province in the hands of a colonel who became the regent of a regime which proclaimed itself independent from the central regime. One by one, all the main Chinese provinces proclaimed their independence and were then led by military commanders chosen by the provincial assemblies who also had the full backing of the new landed nobility. The independence of the provinces was the final step in the new Chinese economic elite's freeing itself from the central regime, thereby expanding its economic and social control over its territory, with no outside interference.

The leaders of the Revolutionary Alliance, commanded by the number two, Huang Hsing, decided to assume the unified command of Hankou where the imperial troops had gathered, the last to be sent by Peking.

Yuan Shih-k'ai was declared prime minister and dictated the conditions for the surrender of the dynasty, by now in decline. Sun then returned to his homeland, arriving in Nanking on 1 January 1912 to proclaim himself interim President of the Republic, although he declared that he would leave the presidency to Yuan, provided the latter supported the Republic. On 12 February 1912, the child Emperor P'u-yi abdicated and Yuan, have settled in Peking on 10 March, became President of the Chinese Republic. So it was that the historical era of heavenly dynasties and absolute rulers came to an end.

3.2 The "Unequal" Treaties

The Boxer Rebellion greatly troubled the foreign powers present in China, since the event in itself had created political instability throughout Asia, as well as pointless bloodshed. For this reason, one by one, the European and American powers, plus Japan, imposed new treaties on China to replace the previous ones. Great Britain made the first move, as it was particularly keen to review the entire customs tariff framework for goods coming into and going out of China. As already mentioned, a tariff was applied at 5% of the average value of the goods; it was increased in 1896, following the heavy Chinese losses due to the war with Japan which led to an increase in the duties on various goods, including wine and tobacco, as well as the introduction of a tax on the opium trade (Francioni 2004, 73–75; Coco 2016).

However, any changes to duties had to be approved by all the other foreign nations. This was precisely where the problem lay, as each national delegation, at a specific International Committee for Tariffs meeting, in which delegates from the USA, France, Great Britain, Germany, Japan and Spain took part, came with different statistics and data for calculating the average value of goods, which provided the rate to be applied as a duty. Based on a Chinese proposal, it was agreed that the trade statistics for 1897–1899 would be used to calculate the average value; this had been a difficult period for trade, characterized by a depreciation in the value of goods. After a long series of bilateral meetings between the Chinese government and those of individual nations, on 29 August 1902 an agreement was drawn up and signed that envisaged new tariffs for the signatories which could be applied to over 700 products, but only if all the signatory nations were in agreement. France, together with other countries, did not accept the agreement, creating a situation in which the merchants of these countries continued to pay 5% ad valorem on the imports of their goods, as they had previously (Francioni 2004, 76–78). Great Britain was the biggest supporter of reviewing the trade treaties, also to "punish" China and its government for its negligence and carelessness in not being quick enough to suppress the Boxer Rebellion.

Great Britain's biggest priority was to have the *likin* abolished; this was a transit duty that increased the tax burden on imported and exported goods. The *likin* was therefore a great hindrance to the circulation of foreign goods, also because the rates differed from province to province, whereas for the Chinese it represented a secure income for paying the troops, the government and the justice system. Furthermore, part of this tax benefited the central government in Peking, which therefore counted on it to fill the state coffers. This tax actually accounted for 14% of revenue in the central budget, immediately behind the revenue from maritime customs, land tax and salt.

The British proposal, whose delegation was led by James Mackay, envisaged the complete abolition of the *likin* and, as compensation for the Chinese, a surcharge of 12.5% ad valorem on goods compared with the prices in the period 1897–1899. The negotiations were very difficult as Mackay's proposal was immediately rejected by the imperial delegates, and he had to travel around almost all the Chinese provinces to convince their governors of the advantages of such a move which, though on the one hand, meant giving up the secure income from the *likin* and on the other hand would allow them to collect higher duties on goods, thanks to the application of a higher rate.

Thus, after gruelling negotiations, the above-mentioned agreement was ratified and came into force on 1 January 1904, although to become fully operative it had to be accepted by all the other "colonial" powers (Francioni 2004, 80–83). It was in any case not in the interests of the other powers to hinder the promotion of a new trade set-up, although naturally each of them tried to "look out for number one". The heaviest criticisms came from Russia which, having obtained transit for the Trans-Siberian line from Amur to Vladivostok, had managed to penetrate the Liao-Tung peninsula and have the Bay of Talien granted for 25 years (Mondaini 1927). Russia was actually operative in these areas, as well as in Manchuria, where the *likin* was not collected as assiduously as in the other provinces and was therefore not interested in supporting the British proposal, which would provide less compensation than if the status quo were maintained.

The protests made by Germany, which used the killing of two German missionaries to justify its occupation of Kiautschou Bay in Shantung in 1898, followed by the granting of a 99-year leasehold of the area, were more of a political than an economic nature. Since Germany had only been informed about the treaty after it was signed, it was critical of Great Britain, accusing it of acting unilaterally without prior consultation of the other great powers and setting itself up as a privileged interlocutor with the Chinese government. Nevertheless, aside from the criticisms of these two countries, the agreement satisfied both sides: with this new treaty, Great Britain and the other foreign power, met the needs of their merchants and industrialists, while China obtained adequate technical compensation, the most important aspect of which was the increase in customs tariffs on many goods.

Article 1 of the new Sino-British treaty envisaged, as well as the abolition of the *likin*, a streamlining of bureaucratic practices, while Articles 5 and 10 introduced facilitations for steam navigation in inland waters, to which specific measures were added for removing obstacles to the passage of steamships on the Canton River, and on the Yangtze between Ichang and Chungking (Francioni 2004, 85). The other important article from a trading point of view was Article 7, relating to the protection of trademarks in China (a very topical subject nowadays, and a source of conflict, now as then, between China and the other nations, with the difference that China is now the hammer rather than the anvil). The other important part of the treaty was that containing clauses that had a profound impact on China's legal structure, as it promoted liberal Western-style reforms for a country whose institutions were still based on the imperial bureaucratic structure. The first step to be taken was to create a single silver currency, given that all over the empire and in the various provinces different types of silver money were used; the foreign powers, in contrast, had gold currencies, which meant that fluctuations in the exchange rate created distortions in commercial and financial transactions. The solution was therefore to create a single silver "currency" for the entire country, but this required the adoption of the gold standard as the monetary regime, a change that the foreign powers were not willing to accept.

The gold standard (pure gold) was an international monetary regime characterized by a pyramidal system with gold at the top and different currencies at the base, which in turn were attached to the precious metal. International financial stability was guaranteed by the fact that, in the event of a disequilibrium in the balance of payments, there was an outflow or an inflow of gold (according to whether a country was in surplus or deficit) (Garofalo 1999, 89–90; Eichengreen 1994; 2004, 39–87). Some countries had a bimetallism system, or rather they used both precious metals, gold and silver, though most used a monometallic system, mainly based on gold.

In the case of China, the dispute arose precisely because it used silver while the foreign powers used gold, with the drawback that if the exchange rate changed,[3] the more precious metal had to be sold at a higher price and the less precious one at a lower price, to restore economic parity between the two metals and to avoid financial instability (Carreras 2002, 328). For this reason, Great Britain and the other countries had no intention of setting the gold standard as the domestic monetary regime in China. Another important article, which though on paper was never actually put into practice, was Article 9, which envisaged the definition of a new regulation for exploiting mineral resources. The mines were located near the major railway lines and without any concessions, the material extracted from them, which was managed by Chinese entrepreneurs, was too expensive for the foreign powers and so they preferred to import coal from the USA and from Great Britain. Nevertheless, it was in China's interest to modernize and further develop the mining sector and to attract foreign investment and capital, but this meant giving up administrative and commercial control of the mines to foreigners, with the result, owing to the presence of foreign personnel on Chinese territory, of an extension of the application of the extraterritoriality principle (Francioni 2004, 86). In addition, this article was strongly opposed by the Germans, the French and above all the Russians, given that in previous years they had obtained concessions in this sector. The first coal mining concession dates back to 1895 and was actually granted to a Franco-British group called the Yunnan Syndicate. This was followed by the Russian Trans-Manchurian railway company, which was allowed to exploit the mines of Fushun, and by Germany, which controlled the mines located alongside the Shantung railway line (Borsa 1977, 261).

One of the articles that had the biggest impact on Chinese business was Article 4, which recognized the right of the Chinese to invest in foreign firms and groups. In practice this was already happening, and the article was merely the legalization of the existing situation. This was a very important clause in the treaty, since it paved the way for the creation of numerous Sino-European public-private capital firms, especially in Hong Kong: in these firms, all partners, including Chinese ones, respected company obligations according to the statute of British firms, and in the event of disputes, the same companies only answered to the British courts of justice and were not subject to the jurisdiction of the Chinese imperial courts. A further two articles should be remembered, which were advantageous for the Chinese. Article 11, which forbade the importing of opium all over China (a historic issue between China and Great Britain which led to the Opium War between China and Great Britain), except for medicinal purposes or if its transport was supervised by the British consulate using operators authorized by the imperial government. Finally, one of the non-commercial articles that actually laid the foundations for a new vision of relations between China and the other countries was Article 12:

> China having expressed a strong desire to reform her judicial system and to bring it into accord with that of the Western nations, Great Britain agrees to give every assistance to such reform, and she will also be prepared to relinquish her extra-territorial rights when she is

[3] The exchange rate is the ratio with which two currencies are exchanged, and is the value of one in terms of the other one. It is decided according to the supply and demand on the currency market.

> satisfied that the state of the Chinese laws, the arrangement for their administration, and other considerations warrant her in so doing. (Francioni 2004, 87–88)

The article invited Great Britain to "help" China build a modern legal system, in order to gradually establish administrative and judicial independence and to fully realize the concept of extraterritoriality. This clause is very important if seen from the point of view of China's internal political frameworks and was of enormous help to the reformists in their battle against the conservative imperial bureaucrats for modernization. The new trade treaty between China and Great Britain was signed on 5 September 1903 and came into force on 28 July; it was warmly welcomed both in China and on the banks of the Thames. The conclusion of the treaty with Great Britain set the standard for drawing up new trade treaties between the "Celestial Empire" and the other foreign powers present there.

In 1903 the USA and Japan also concluded new trade treaties with China. Great Britain had assumed the position of a privileged interlocutor with the Chinese government, being the first to inaugurate and ask for a review of the treaties. The USA also contributed greatly by adopting an Open Door policy to address the policy on concessions and on spheres of influence; the Open Door policy consisted of convincing all the foreign powers to accept equal treatment throughout China, so as to guarantee equal access for all of them to trade and finance. This move was intended on the one hand, to limit the dominance of Great Britain and France and on the other hand, to achieve an imperialism based on economic hegemony through the full opening of international trade. As regards the USA, they almost entirely accepted the clauses included in the British treaty, and also requested protection for the Protestant religious missions (given that the protestant movement and religious sentiment were very strong in the USA at that time, just as they are today). In addition, they managed to obtain benefits and privileges for American diplomatic representatives all over China.

From a commercial point of view, trade between the USA and China had been promising following the Treaty of Wangxia in 1844, but the American Civil War brought it to a standstill, to the point that American exports only accounted for 3% of all China's foreign trade until the end of the 1880s. Nevertheless, it was in the US interests to make more headway in China; after their victorious war with Spain for the conquest of Cuba and the annexation of the Philippines, the USA was by now a real "Asian power".

In contrast to European imperialism, the American version was not intended to conquer Chinese territory, preferring to focus on establishing commercial influence in order to increase exports, a process helped in 1893 by the establishment of two large industrial groups: the "American China Development Company" and the "American Asiatic Association", financed by American industrialists and financiers. In order to put the "Open Door" policy into practice, during the negotiations with the imperial delegates, the USA requested the opening of the naval ports facing Manchuria. This inevitably created friction with Russia which had obtained the concession in the Manchu territory to build the biggest railway in the country; this was the Trans-Siberian, which had total control there since the early years of the twentieth century, when the Tsar's troops had occupied it during the war against the Boxers. Moreover, Russia also controlled the naval base of Port Arthur and it was only the joint pressure of Great Britain and Japan that led to the drawing up of an agreement in 1903 that achieved the total evacuation by the Russians from this area and the restoration of full sovereignty to Peking (Francioni 2004, 95).

On the one hand, the Chinese did not want to upset the Americans, but on the other hand neither did they wish to undermine their relations with the Russians and completely renege on the concessions policy. The USA moved at three levels: with the imperial delegates in Shanghai for trade, in Peking for the concession for opening the Manchu ports and in Moscow with the Tsar himself. A solution was found in the form of an acceptable compromise: Russia accepted the opening of the ports in exchange for the USA giving up Harbin, a strategic area for the development of a railway system in Manchuria.

China was confronted with these conditions and could do nothing about them and so it agreed to sign the treaty with the USA on 8 October 1903 which, as mentioned previously, aside from obtaining the opening of various new ports to trade, essentially copied many of the provisions in the Sino-British treaty. The agreement with the US paved the way for the beginning of talks to revise the trade treaty with Japan, the negotiations for which were, however, suspended because of the Russo-Japanese war for the control of the Liaotung peninsula and the railways of southern Manchuria which fell under Japanese control at the end of the war. The American government declared neutrality, but acted in such a way as to foster Japanese victory, essentially because the Japanese government had taken out several loans in the USA and victory for Japan would weaken the presence and dampen the ambitions of Russia in that area. Nevertheless, even though there was a war, on 8 October 1903 Japan also signed a new treaty providing for the abolition of the *likin* in exchange for a greater freedom of navigation on China's inland waterways, help for Japanese entrepreneurs in renting warehouses for their business and the opening of Manchu ports (Japan had in fact given its full support to the "Open Door" policy) (Francioni 2004, 102–103).

3.2.1 Portugal and Germany

Following the lead of the three main treaty powers (the USA, Great Britain and France), Portugal and Germany also decided to sit down with the Chinese to review their politic and trade relations.

Portugal had obtained full sovereignty over the territory of Macao in 1887, and the negotiations aimed above all to establish clear and definitive limits to the territory under their control.

The negotiations were held between February and October 1902, but the situation was more difficult than expected, so much so that Castello Blanco, the Portuguese government's foreign affairs delegate, made do with drawing up a commercial agreement with the Chinese which stated that some Portuguese goods would be exempted from payment of customs duties and promised that the concession to build a railway line between Macao and Canton would be granted to a mixed Sino-Portuguese industrial group (Francioni 2004, 106). From a purely commercial point of view, the most important articles of the treaty, concluded in Shanghai on 11 November 1903, concerned the abolition of the *likin*, the prohibition on the opium trade, the forming of public-private trading companies, and the protection of trademarks. The last country in terms of time to take advantage of the opportunity to renegotiate its agreements with China was Germany.[4]

Germany was a country with significant interests in China and was the most vocal critic of the British proposal to abolish the *likin*. German trade was, however, expanding in the Celestial Empire, though not to the extent that it was justified in starting disputes with other countries. Germany's proposals aimed above all at obtaining the concession for German traders of the "right to reside in all the areas of the empire where they were authorized to dock their steamships for navigating the inland waterways" (Francioni 2004, 109). This point could not be accepted by China's imperial delegates, for one simple reason. If the German proposal had been accepted, all of the Kaiser's subjects would have been able to live in any part of the empire, carry out their trade, rent warehouses, shops and equipment, under the protection of the German government. Owing to the favoured nation clause, this would have created an extremely dangerous situation for China, as it broadened the application of the extraterritoriality principle to other countries as well, a principle that China was laboriously trying to remove from its legal system. It can be said that, in the two-year period 1902–1903, the three powers most present in China, namely Great Britain, the USA and Japan, had obtained new treaties that were favourable to them from a trading point of view, and they pushed the other treaty powers to follow in their footsteps. By reviewing its tariffs and accepting some clauses, if on the one hand China was accepting a greater influence of foreign states on its territory, then on the other hand, it was heading towards to a more reformist organization of the country in terms of its international political and commercial relations.

Nevertheless, these treaties can be defined as unequal, if examined from a Chinese point of view. There were foreigners working in China as if they were semi-colonialists, and they checked and interfered in almost all matters regarding local government and the management of public services. The marine customs and almost all public offices were staffed by foreigners employed and paid by the Chinese government, and the customs duties collected and other taxes on goods were mainly used by the government to pay off foreign loans and war indemnities (Fairbank 1988, 225). In 1905, Italy also set up diplomatic relations, a little later than the other countries, in order to have the old trade treaty revised that had been concluded by Admiral Arminjon in 1866.

[4]See Coco (2016) for the interesting and original documentation on German colonialism between 1897 and 1914 and the original documentation on German colonialism between 1897 and 1914.

3.3 The First Chinese Republic

In the early years of the Republic the central government's main priority was to keep the country united so as to be able to defend itself.

The Republic of 1911 inherited the vast territory that the Manchu empire had conquered over the course of centuries, and it could not afford to lose or relinquish any of it, because if this were to happen, the outside world would see it as a sign of weakness.

Nevertheless, Mongolia and Tibet broke away from the Republic. China had always taken a colonial stance towards these two peoples, considering them as minorities, yet it was unable to exercise complete control over either of them. As far as Mongolia was concerned, the Russians had a very strong commercial influence there, and it was not in their interests for the central authorities of Peking to have total control of that area; in 1915, a compromise was reached following a series of negotiations, in which China maintained a kind of formal authority over the region, while Russia obtained not only economic advantages but also a kind of protectorate there, and set up a Mongolian army to defend it that was trained by the Russian military (Fairbank 1988, 214–215).

In Tibet, instead there was a theocratic government headed by the Dalai Lama,[5] who was driven out following the invasion by the Chinese army in 1910. However, the Dalai Lama returned to his country in 1911 and proclaimed its independence from China. Tibet had always been formally controlled by Great Britain, which helped to draw up a compromise between the government in Peking and the theocratic government: Tibet obtained local autonomy and recognition of its independence by Great Britain but not by China, which claimed sovereignty over the region. In this way, Great Britain was able to establish a basis for an increase in trade with Tibet, while China only kept formal authority over the region which was only placed under the total control of the Chinese with the advent of Mao Tse-tung's People's Republic of China.

From a trade point of view, in Republican China, the control of navigation along the rivers belonged almost exclusively to the British, whereas oil, which was a precious commodity as it provided lighting for the peasants in the countryside, was mainly distributed by Texaco and Royal Dutch Shell, an Anglo-Dutch cartel.[6]

The other article for mass consumption guaranteed by foreign countries was tobacco, and competition in this sector was above all between British firms and the Nanyang Brothers, a company of south-east Asia. Yet one of the biggest problems for Yuan, President of the Republic, was China's institutional framework. Up

---

[5]The Dalai Lama is the supreme temporal leader of Tibet, and the highest spiritual authority of Tibetan Buddhism. He is also the leader of the current Tibetan government in exile.

[6]It started as The Texas Fuel Company, founded in 1901 in Beaumont, Texas; The Royal Dutch/Shell Group was created in 1907. The Royal Dutch Oil Company (legal name in Dutch, NV Koninklijke Nederlandsche Petroleum Maatschappij) and The "Shell" Transport and Trading Company plc, merged to compete against the oil giant of that era, Standard Oil. They were part of those Western multinationals called "Seven Sisters" which had an undisputed hegemony in this field until the second half of the twentieth century (Pollard 2004, 242–243).

until then, the Emperor had been seen as the Son of Heaven, occupying all the positions of responsibility: head of the government, high priest of China's cults, patron of the arts and of literature, and supreme military commander. However, in 1912 the population was aware that this form of government was dated and needed to move, albeit gradually, towards the creation of a Western-style institutional set-up. This is why the first political parties came into being in this period, and began to be considered important, although at that time they were just groups that gathered around a leading figure.

In 1912, Yuan gave T'ang Shao-i a mandate to form a government: the ministries, however, immediately declared themselves loyal to the President and not to the head of the government. T'ang, who had neither substantial resources nor a stable organization, resigned from his mandate and a presidential-style government was created. One of the first parties to appear on the political scene, which would go on to be very successful, was that formed by Sung Chiao-jen, who was inspired by Jeffersonian principles and merged his Revolutionary Alliance with other parties, creating the Chinese nationalist party, known as the Kuomintang (Fairbank 1988, 219). Between 1912 and 1913 the first elections were held, which saw the participation, as an electorate with the right to vote, of a number of voters equal to 4 for every thousand of the population. Most of the seats went to the Kuomintang, and thanks to this results Sun believed he could use constitutional means to limit Yuan's dominance Yuan. The latter had anticipated Sun's moves and carried out a series of antidemocratic acts: he sacked the servicemen loyal to Sun, outlawed the Kuomintang and dissolved most of the provincial and local assemblies, instigated a reign of terror and in 1914 he even proclaimed himself Emperor. By now, however, the Chinese ruling class, the intellectuals and the military, as well as the most powerful provincial lords, could not tolerate the return of an imperial government, especially one that dealt in terror and death, and so they organized an armed revolt to nip Yuan's intentions in the bud, and he died alone in June 1916 (Fairbank 1988, 221).

The reason for all the opposition parties merging against Yuan was his acceptance of Japan's "Twenty-one Demands" which, were they to be accepted would turn China into a kind of Japanese semi-colony. Yuan played for time, given the popular revolts that had sprung up, but he eventually signed the treaty, thereby signing his own death warrant. With the revolution of 1911 and the birth of the Republic, as we have seen, a phase of political division began, between those who favoured a presidential style of government and those who were pushing for a framework that guaranteed power and legitimacy to the parties (Schmidt-Glintzer 2005, 238). It was during this phase that the warlords pushed their way in and increasingly assumed power.

Their power grew following the death of Yuan, and up until 1928, the year when the Kuomintang was reunited, China was highly fragmented from a political point of view, with each territory ruled by a military commander, who in turn made and broke alliances to create military coalitions to defeat their rivals: the strength of these military lords lay in the fact that they had complete control over the local armies. This was the result of the army reforms that had taken place between the end of the nineteenth and the beginning of the twentieth centuries. In this period the central government in Peking limited itself to guaranteeing public services, such as the postal service, and maintaining its diplomatic representation abroad.

As we have said, the warlords kept their power thanks to their armies, which moved around above all along the waterways and the railways, and acts of war mainly involved the populations they encountered along the way. Such conflicts were often financed with the taxes levied from the same people against whom they waged war. These incidents rarely occurred in the urban and modernized areas of China though, and their spell of dominance was brief and limited to the rural areas, although it would have significant consequences for the country as a whole.

Once they had conquered a territory and were bolstered by military support, the warlords' main priority was to make friends with the most powerful men and administrators there, to the extent that public sector corruption reached unprecedented levels in that period. The money and resources from taxes and duties were not spent on public services or investment: dams were not built, long-term investment was in decline, the opium trade flourished again, inflation rose, leading to a fall in the currency's purchasing power, especially for the less well-off, and living conditions for those in occupied territories deteriorated over time (Fairbank 1988, 229). Between 1916 and 1928 roughly two hundred generals managed to create havoc and unrest throughout China. Their ascent to power was facilitated above all by their being decorated servicemen, which helped greatly in the recruitment of troops and soldiers and by the exponential increase in weapons thanks to the development of new technology. The other reason that allowed them to extend their power was the political instability reigning in the central institutions which did not ensure the political unity of the nation owing to the fratricidal power struggles between the various factions.

At the time of the warlords' rule, China was hit by an insidious civil war, full of intrigues, betrayals and ambushes among the generals, all of which simply depleted its economic resources and led to the destruction of towns and villages (Corradini 1969, 253). Nonetheless, the central government of Peking was the only one that was legally recognized by the foreign powers, and it was this government that in 1917 took part in the First World War and then at the end of the war took its place with the other victors at the negotiating table. At the Peace Conference held immediately after the end of the First World War in Versailles, as one of the winning nations China thought it would be able to settle some scores with certain foreign powers. Specifically, China asked for total sovereignty over the areas that had been ceded to Japan by Yuan through his acceptance of Japan's "Twenty-one Demands", together with the abolition of the Sino-Japanese Treaty of 1915.

None of China's requests were accepted, however, and the news of its diplomatic failure provoked serious protests from university students in Peking, who asked for the delegates to be recalled from Versailles. This occurred on 4 May 1919, an important day in Chinese history, as it represented the moment when China's culture and its ruling class were truly renewed (Corradini 1969, 254). The students' protests of the were flanked by those of the university professors and of famous scholars and men of letters. The latter contributed to the founding of magazines that blew the winds of social and cultural change to the masses, a change badly needed by China. An article by Li Ta-chao, a history professor, appeared in the magazine "The New Youth" in 1920 in which, in part by analysing the October Revolution in Russia, he explained Marxism and how its doctrine could take root and be effective in a country like China. Communist ideals began to be understood and accepted by a growing number of people, to the point that the Chinese Communist Party on 1 July 1921, in Shanghai. After Yuan's rule was over, the group that seemed most ready to take power was the Kuomintang, together with its leader, Sun Yat-sen. In 1917, Sun was too weak to oppose the warlords and had accepted help from the communists, including funds and weapons supplied by the Soviet Union, which also sent military trainers and political advisors to Peking, and the Kuomintang became increasingly similar to the Soviet Union's Communist Party, in terms of its bureaucratic and internal structure. After years of preparation, the nationalist party was ready to launch an attack on the generals of the north, when Sun suddenly died, leaving the party's leadership in the hands of General Chang Kai-shek. In 1927, the new leader started a great expeditionary campaign northwards, in order to reconquer the territories occupied by the warlords. His army managed to overcome the northern generals' local armies, but just before it entered Shanghai, he broke the pact with the communists, withdrew all their mandates and expelled the soviet advisors and military representatives. Although the capital was also moved to Nanking, and Chiang Kai-shek's government was recognized by all the foreign powers, his victory was more formal than substantial, and in fact, several generals and northern lords, despite having recognized the new government, still held onto power and managed the administration and political affairs of their territories (Corradini 1969, 257).

In the years that followed, the civil war became total and was fought all over China, involving the nationalist party on one side and the communist party on the other. After twenty years of fierce fighting, with blood spilt on both sides, of anarchy and chaos following violent battles, with thousands of men moving from the Kuomintang to the communist party, on 1 October 1949 the Communist leader Mao Tse-tung proclaimed the birth of the People's Republic of China, and declared Chiang Kai-shek's government, established in the meantime in Taiwan, to be illegitimate.

Chapter 4
Italy in China: 1861–1919

Abstract This chapter will examine the first commercial solutions between Italy and China and the influence of Italian politics. The analysed period is particularly significant for the history of Italy because it is rich in important events and phenomena; it is also called the Belle Époque. This term indicates the European historical, socio-cultural and artistic period that goes from the last twenty years of the nineteenth century to the beginning of the First World War. Moreover, from an economic point of view the period between 1896 and 1907 is called the Giolittian period. According to Gerschenkron's estimates (1962; Il Problema storico dell'arretratezza economica. Bellknap, Cambridge, Mass, 1965), in this period the average rate of growth for Italian industrial production went from 0.3 to 6.7% and then fell, between 1908 and 1913 to 2.4%. According to the Fenoaltea calculations (La crescita industriale delle regioni d'Italia dall'Unità alla grande guerra: una prima stima per gli anni censuari. Bank of Italy, Rome, 2001), the annual growth rates, again for industrial production and for the same periods, were, respectively, 7.6 and 2.3%. Istat calculated figures for 0.5 and 1.5%. Leaving aside a discussion of the reasons for the various degrees of reliability of these indices, as well as those of the contrasting historiographical uses that have been made of them in order to theorize or not on the existence of a take-off in the process of industrialization of the country, it is a known fact that the productive expansion in the Giolittian age (about 1901–1914) had no precedent with respect to that of the post-unification decades, despite the setback of 1907. Notwithstanding the persistence of protectionist duties, whose incidence was however attenuated by the increase in prices, progress in transport, the new lines of exchange, the reduction of freight rates and the revision of trade treaties all supported the expansion phase, as did the increase in international trade. It was in this climate that Italy, in order not to be outdone by the other capitalist powers, initiated its first commercial treaties with China.

4.1 Post-unification Italy: A Summary

Following its unification, Italy presented itself to the outside world with the institutional framework, agricultural equipment and industrial plants of a backward country compared with the other European countries, with a mentality that was still parochial

D. Strangio, *Italy-China Trade Relations*, Studies in Economic History,
https://doi.org/10.1007/978-3-030-39084-6_4

and provincial, and in a state of national unity that was more on paper than in practice. From a social point of view, the city was the administrative centre and the location for weekly markets and was limited to the exchange of goods between the rural population and the townsfolk. It had lost the powers of attraction typical of the sixteenth century, to the extent that immigration from the country to the city had fallen significantly; the fact that births outnumbered deaths was explained by famines and infant mortality and the consequent need to repopulate in order to have manpower to work in the country.

The underdevelopment of Italy compared with the other European countries, especially Great Britain and France, the most advanced countries at that time in terms of growth and modernization, was also seen in the state of its infrastructures. Piedmont and Tuscany had more railway lines than the other regions and therefore had adequate links for transporting both goods and people between the provincial capitals and the smaller towns.

South of Tuscany, however, there were very few railway lines, and prior to 1861, there were no rail links at all in central and southern Italy (Giuntini 1991, 2001; Maggi 2005, 18–21). Yet the main problem was to create a sense of common purpose and a national sentiment among all Italian people, because as Massimo D'Azeglio had said: "We have made Italy; now we must make Italians" (Montanelli 2003a).

Italy was divided, not only in economic terms but also by traditions, particularities and the strong vested interests of various social groups. The best way to overcome these divisions was to create transport links between the three areas of Italy: north, centre and south. In order to achieve this, a series of public works to create railway and road infrastructures had to be undertaken. As regards numbers, in the years 1861–1866, roughly 800 million lire were spent on building railway lines, as well as 136 million lire on road projects, especially in the centre and the south, and over 60 million lire on hydraulic projects and land reclamation. Although building railways from the Alps to the more southern regions brought benefits in the short term, what was lacking was a driving force to make Italy a leader in industry, on a par with Great Britain and France, especially in metalworking and mechanical engineering (Luzzatto 1968, 16–21).

In the early years of the Kingdom, Italy's rulers had to face two other problems in addition to those mentioned previously: banditry (Benigno 2015), especially in southern Italy, which could have dealt a mortal blow to the work of unification under way, and Italy's financial situation at that time. According to Carlo De Cesare, a Ministry of Finance official, in 1859 public debt in the Kingdom of Sardinia and in the Kingdom of Naples and Sicily stood at 2446 million lire, mostly due to investments in railways during the period of Cavour, war expenses and the indemnity owed to Austria.[1]

In the first five years following unification, despite the increase in taxes, revenues increased from 480 to 645 million lire, against an outlay of expenditure that increased from 926 to 1338 million lire in the same period; the resulting deficit, though increasing at a slower rate, of 721 million lire, was very high for that period (Luzzatto 1968,

[1]On long-term trends in public debt, see among others Postigliola and Strangio (2017, 313–330).

41). Yet the reason for the negative situation from both a financial and an economic point of view was found in the choices made in order to remedy the budget deficit. Italy's rulers adopted two strategies at the same time: recourse to foreign loans and selling state property. In order to encourage subscribers to purchase Italian public debt securities, high premiums and interest were granted that raised the debt by a further 2660 million lire, while only just over 1800 million went into the state coffers. Most of the securities were sold on the London and Paris stock exchanges, recourse to foreign loans, while on the one hand it guaranteed funds for building works, above all for the railways and freeing up resources in other sectors, and on the other hand, it increased public debt still further, with serious consequences at economic and industrial level.

The other problem, which was not clearly understood at that time, was that this considerable sale of public securities would make the newly created state of Italy reliant on foreign countries, especially with regard to specific economic policy choices (Fenoaltea 2006).

The other method used to decrease public debt was the sale and concession of state property. By expropriating the Church's goods after the fall of the Papal States, Italy had acquired considerable wealth in the form of lands and buildings (property of the Papal States). Most of these assets were sold immediately in order to acquire the money needed for rebalancing the public finances. In the transport sector too, and in this case in order to free itself from an extremely expensive and burdensome administration, the State disposed of several stretches of railway track, especially the Ligurian-Piedmontese network inherited from the Savoy state, which was sold to the Società Alta Italia (northern Italy's rail company) for 200 million lire. As far as inland waterways and irrigation canals were concerned, particularly in Piedmont, the state administration was convinced that they could also be more easily exploited by private industry.

An opportunity for this came with the realization of the Cavour Canal project. An English company was engaged to build and manage the canal, for a fee of 20 million lire, and it was also given the use of all the state canals and all their branches and outbuildings, including factories, mills and rice husking machines (Luzzatto 1968, 35–36; Cohen and Federico 2001). Most of Italy's revenues at that time, apart from the collection of duties and taxes, came from the monopolies on salt, tobacco and lottery games, which had a single tariff all over Italy in 1864 except for Sicily. The tariff was raised that same year and over the next three years increased state revenues by 70 million lire net.

Following unification, agriculture was the source of livelihood for almost the entire Italian population (Federico 1979, 1994a). From a statistical point of view, at least up until the first half of the 1870s there are no accurate and documentable data, especially regarding the increase in the production of crops and cereals. With specific reference to Italy's agrarian landscape at that time, we can examine what Stefano Iacini wrote in his *Inchiesta Agraria* in 1877:

> We still find several different agricultural Italies, not only because of what they produce, which will always be the case, but also because they still have almost exactly the same form, the same appearance and the same pattern, instilled and impressed upon them by the

> political, administrative and social orders from which they arose, even though those orders have disappeared. (Zamagni 1990, 74)

Italy's agricultural diversity can be explained by looking at four areas of the country: the Po Valley, extensively irrigated, where cereals, rice, beetroot and forage were cultivated and which had a high yield per hectare; the northern hills, in Liguria and the surrounding areas, which grew specialized crops such as grapes, olives for oil and fruit and were also profitable; the hills and plains of central and southern Italy where above all cereals, vines, citrus fruits, pulses and vegetables were cultivated, but with a lower yield than in the north; and lastly, the mountains, which covered over a third of Italy's agricultural surface area and where it was impossible to achieve adequate and profitable yields, either from a qualitative or from a quantitative point of view.

As far as how the land was worked and organized is concerned, there were three different typologies: smallholdings, especially in Piedmont and Abruzzo, which were essentially a form of subsistence farming, supported by employed labour and which also included farms specializing in vineyards or in growing vegetables. There were leases, especially in the Po Valley, which was a kind of speculative model, consisting in the renting out of land by the owner at a fairly low rate, but the tenants were obliged to plant certain crops which had to be handed over to the landlord at the end of the contract. Tenants had employees who were hired on yearly contracts, but most workers were labourers hired and paid by the day. Finally, sharecropping, which consisted of a contract between the landowner and the tenant, which meant sharing the harvest equally between them, with the means of production almost always belonging to the landowner (Zamagni 1990, 90–91). Conditions for workers in the fields were very hard, and wages were extremely low, especially during the winter months, where women and children (who were also used as labour in the country) were paid a pittance of 50 cents a day, at a time when a kilo of bread cost 58 cents.[2] Worse still were the living conditions for the peasants in almost all the regions of Italy. The "luckiest" families lived huddled up, together with their livestock, in one-room houses with no light or air, while others lived in huts with straw roofs and no flooring (Luzzatto 1968, 102).

In addition, it can be seen how, in this period, the agrarian situation in some parts of Italy was static and showed very little sign of progress with regard to equipment and farming techniques. It was only in the northern plains that iron ploughs and steam threshers began to be used in the 1870s, although they were not always used to the same extent in this area. The crop rotations were still the same as in previous centuries: forage crops were scarce and the plots of land were mainly used as pasture. Chemical fertilizers were used in the Alps, but nowhere else in Italy, as the other regions used animal manure, although not the south, as the long periods of drought meant that arable crops and therefore intensive grazing were not possible, so rather than using animal manure, stubble was burned instead. From an institutional point of view, in order to improve farming practices and increase productivity, several laws on

[2]On wages, see Zamagni (1976, 538–539; 2002), Vannutelli (1961), Favero (2010) and Di Martino and Vasta (2017).

loans for agriculture were approved, which consisted in donations of money at low interest rates with the aim of replacing common loans such as mortgages and also to eradicate usury. The idea of a law on agricultural credit began to circulate among the institutions at the end of the 1860s, and a law was then approved on 21 June 1869 although it did not have the hoped-for results. It was only in 1887 that a law was approved that provided a greater incentive for setting up departments for agricultural credit in the Casse di Risparmio (savings banks), but only six departments were actually created. It was not until the early years of the twentieth century, and thanks to the special laws passed for the south, that measures were approved for facilitating the opening of stand-alone credit institutions, as a way to compensate for the lack of local initiatives and the failure of the grain mountains.[3] Progress in wheat cultivation, the basic seed for the production of other products and crops, was minimal in Italy from unification to the end of the nineteenth century. Between 1860 and 1870, Italy increased its grain production, according to statistics that are still uncertain and not accurate, by over 42%; yet after the mid-1870s, there was a steady and continuous regression, with a decrease of 15% recorded until the years 1894–1898.

Other elements that help us understand and corroborate the idea of a minimal increase in agricultural production in Italy are the data on customs statistics, which show that grain imports had reached a ceiling of 4.5 million quintals in the three-year period 1863–1865, while over the whole of the 1870s, with an increase in the population, they had gone down to between 2.5 and 3.5 million quintals (Luzzatto 1968, 95–99). As far as the trade policy of the new Kingdom of Italy is concerned, in the twenty years from 1862 to 1882 we can see in Table 4.1 that both imports and exports increased, but with a surplus in exports only in the year 1871.

Despite the difficulties encountered in the early years, from a trading point of view Italy experienced a constant growth over time, with an increase in foreign trade of more than three-fifths from 1863 to 1876. This increase was due above all to the introduction of the forced tender. On 1 January, faced with the risk of financial disaster, the government approved a decree declaring the inconvertibility of banknotes into gold. This led to the introduction of paper money and ensured the State the possibility of making payments rapidly simply by printing banknotes (Stringher 1881).

The effect of introducing forced tender led to a fall in imports in the period 1866–1871 compared with the previous years, and at the same time, there was an increase in exports, which rose from 558 million lire in 1865 to 1075 million lire in 1871, thereby improving the trade balance, which showed a surplus of 114 million lire that same year.

The effects of forced tender came to an end in 1873, while exports reached new highs after 1878, when a new customs tariff was set, which in turn brought the

[3]The grain mountains had the purpose of advancing seeds to farmers at a moderate interest rate. They were created to combat usury, but if that was in some way their initial function, they quickly fell into the hands of the "squires", who introduced oppressive systems into local governments, making use of them to increase their power over the farmers (see Checcoli 2015).

Table 4.1 Kingdom of Italy—imports and exports (1861–1882)

	Imports	Exports	Import surplus
1862	830	577	253
1863	902	634	268
1864	984	573	411
1865	965	558	407
1866	870	618	252
1867	886	740	146
1868	897	787	110
1869	937	792	145
1870	896	756	140
1871	961	1075	−114
1872	1182	1162	20
1873	1261	1131	130
1874	1295	978	317
1875	1207	1022	185
1876	1307	1208	99
1877	1141	934	207
1878	1062	1021	41
1879	1252	1072	180
1880	1187	1104	83
1881	1240	1165	75
1882	1227	1152	75

Source The data in the table are official data on special foreign trade, taken from Capanna and Messeri (1940)

increase in imports to a halt. Grain was Italy's main import, but coal and coke were also important.

In the early years of the Kingdom, the share of cotton imports was modest, although it recorded an increase after 1866, when Italy purchased this raw material directly from cotton-producing countries such as the USA, India and Egypt. This was one of the reasons that pushed Italy to establish diplomatic and trade relations with China, a country rich in raw materials for Italy's spinning industry. As far as heavy industry was concerned, imports were above all semi-finished products such as cast iron, steel, rolled sections and rails, but their share was minimal, and the level of exports was also low in that sector.

The value of the imports in the twenty-year period analysed was therefore greater than that of exports by around one-fifth.

Exports were mainly semi-finished products such as raw silk, two-thirds of which went to France, minerals such as sulphur, and marbles, which were useful for the activity of Italy's merchant navy, and agricultural products such as olive oil, wine, citrus and dried fruits. This shows how products under the heading of "exports" were basic ones, and bears witness to how little progress was made in industrial production at that time in Italy (Luzzatto 1968, 146–151). On the eve of unification, Italy was extremely backward industrially speaking compared with the main European countries. The main obstacles to full industrial development in Italy stemmed above all from the restricted nature of the domestic market due to the difficulties in transport and the deficiencies in infrastructure between the various Italian regions, despite the fact that great efforts were made after 1861 to abolish internal customs.

The obstacles were, on the one hand, the high cost of money, which made investments non-profitable, especially private ones, and on the other hand the almost total lack of fossil fuels, which were only found in Val d'Aosta, Umbria and Tuscany, and were for the most part imported from abroad, which had a serious impact on the state budget (Luzzatto 1968, 116–117). The first steps towards true industrialization took place between unification and the First World War, above all in the north-western triangle (Fenoaltea 2006).

Between 1871 and 1911, overall production grew in all the regions, except for Basilicata, but the growth rates differed; in the long term, they were highest in the north-west triangle, where industrial output grew by 3.2% in Piedmont, 3.6% in Lombardy and 4.7% in Liguria. They were followed by Tuscany, Emilia Romagna and Lazio and then by all the southern regions and the islands, where growth was slower. By comparing the trends in 1871, it can be seen that industrial output in Lombardy was 14 times higher than that in Basilicata. In the intervening years in Piedmont, Liguria and Lombardy, the share of industrial output was in continuous growth from 1871 to 1911, while the share was in decline in the Marches, Abruzzo, Basilicata and Calabria. This macroregional differentiation meant that there was no "unification effect" to be seen that could draw together the north and the south of Italy in terms of industrial growth and development.

From an economic policy point of view, the 1880s saw a move towards protectionism that favoured industry in northern Italy; in addition, the fall in transport costs, also due to regional specialization, supports the hypothesis that the minor railway lines built between 1880 and 1895 were more important economically speaking than the major peninsular lines built immediately after unification (Fenoaltea 2001, 11–12).

The key aspect of post-unification industrial development was that it developed outside the north-western triangle, where up until Lombardy had enjoyed exclusive industrial supremacy. However, a decade after unification, Italy's industrial map still displayed a traditional type of economy, and in the centre, there were no factories, which were half and fly for export to foreign markets and which needed guaranteed energy and transport infrastructures, but above all, there were artisan and manufacturing workshops that marketed products especially to Italy's elite. From the point of view of industrial segmentation, in the post-unification years, the industrial structure was designed to satisfy primary needs at national level. The food industries accounted for around a fifth of the total, followed by textiles, clothing, wood, minerals and hides and then by engineering, manufacturing, utilities and extractive industries. Over time, there would be a decline in the food sector with a growth above all in the technical and mechanical industries.

In general terms, the industrial structures of the various regions are similar, in part thanks to the high costs of transport that hindered specialization and exchanges. There were greater differences with regard to the extractive industry and less significant differences in the building sector, with a relatively high weight especially in Basilicata, Calabria, Puglia, Lazio and Tuscany. There were marked regional differences in the utilities sector, with a low incidence in the southern regions, due in particular to the lack of hydroelectric resources and municipal services in that part of Italy.

There were strong similarities in the manufacturing sector among the various regions, headed by the food industry and followed by the mechanical industry and agriculture (Fenoaltea 2001, 16–20). The mechanical industry was extremely backward in 1871, essentially because its factories were still at artisan level or were even like cottage industries. Some progress had been made in the textile industry, especially in the field of spinning, while the silk industry still functioned in a rural way, as steam had not yet replaced the open fire in the heating processes. The proclamation of the Kingdom was swiftly followed by a serious crisis in the textile industry caused by various factors, including a disease in silkworms that pushed Italy to look for new and similar raw materials in Asian countries (Rosa 1868; Federico 1988, 1994b; Federico et al. 2011; Chilosi and Federico 2013, 58 sgg.; Marcelli 2013, 38–39).[4] The consequences of the American Civil War were even more serious after 1861, as the blockading of the southern ports meant it was impossible to export raw cotton to Europe (Luzzatto 1968, 126–129). The situation changed over time, thanks to improvements in transport and the lower relative costs, to the growing specialization and to the industrialization that took place at varying speeds throughout the various regions (Daniele and Malanima 2011, 65–82; Di Martino and Vasta 2017; Felice 2007). In the first decade of the twentieth century, while the agricultural and food industries were still paramount in the south, the Milan-Turin-Genoa triangle distinguished itself by specializing in the textile and mechanical industries, which were double the size of the food industry. It can be stated that, while in the first decade following unification the industrial situation was not very different from pre-unification times, after 1871 there was a growth in industrialization, though varying from region to region and from province to province. This was due to various factors, such as the completion of the railway network and the decline in recourse to loans to reduce the deficit in the government budget, also thanks to the coverage provided by the revenue

[4]Italy's main trading partners were, in the first decades after unification, Great Britain, from which a large part of coal came, and above all France, with which trade was intense and covers a wide range of goods. Following the "trade war" with France, which determines a strong contraction of trade towards the Alps, the role of Great Britain in the field of imports of primary products was consolidated and Germany's role for manufactured goods emerged. Despite the downsizing of trade flows during and after the First World War, Germany was once again the first trading partner, and in the second half of the 1930s, it was by far the main supplier of coal. From the beginning of the twentieth century, trade with the American continent increased, also due to the effect of migration flows from Italy and the USA, at least until the 1929 crisis, thus becoming one of the main trading partners for the Italian economy (Federico et al. 2011, 50).

from selling ecclesiastical and state property, thereby making resources available for investment in industry and infrastructure (Luzzatto 1968, 130).

4.2 The First Steps in the Far East

At the dawn of the nineteenth century, the pre-unification Italian states, which were economically inferior to the other European countries, hardly took part at all in international trade, preferring trade routes in the Mediterranean, the Black Sea and the Atlantic, and ships flying the Italian flag almost never sailed to the Far East (Mancini 1987, 402–403). The only states that had consulates in Chinese territory, specifically in Macao and Canton, were the Kingdom of Sardinia and the Kingdom of Sicily. Their presence was, however, more official than operational, given that the two kingdoms had no trade relations with China and had no national interests and very few compatriots there to need protection. In contrast, as far as the new Kingdom of Italy was concerned, it was important to try and establish a diplomatic foothold there as soon as possible in the countries of the Far East as well.

Camillo Benso di Cavour took up the initiative to extend Sardinia's consular network in China 1857 (Mancini 1987), and after an accurate examination of the situation, in 1866 the decision was made not to reopen the consulate in Canton but to establish a new consulate general in Shanghai, which at that time was one of China's most important ports and the nerve centre of the silk trade. In addition, Italy also managed to obtain a small piece of land at the beginning of the twentieth century, namely the concession of Tientsin.

Prior to the opening of the consulate general in Shanghai, in 1863 the idea took shape of sending a diplomatic mission to safeguard Italian traders in China and Japan; it was to be an Italian delegation headed by Cristoforo Negri, who was head of all the consulates at the Ministry of Foreign Affairs. The main goal of the mission was to increase business activities linked to the silk trade, since a disease of silkworms called pébrine had swept through Italy, causing considerable damage in the Veneto and in Lombardy; this meant it was necessary to import raw materials from the east to regenerate the national silkworm egg stocks (Rosa 1868). The disease began to spread through Europe between the end of the 1850s and the early 1860s; Italy was the leading producer of cocoons, with a total of around 60 million kg, the quantity and quality of which declined as the disease spread. In the five years from 1862 to 1866, cocoons and raw silks had to be imported, especially from countries as yet untouched by pébrine (Borsa 1961, 21).

These imports had to be made by launching an ad hoc company set up in Bergamo, tasked with buying silkworm eggs from the Far East, a company whose partners were supposed to be part of the government delegation led by Negri.[5] The delegation

[5]Historical Diplomatic Archives of the Ministry of Foreign Affairs, Ministry of Foreign Affairs Writings: Kingdom of Italy 1861–1887, Busta 18 Fascicolo 7, Letter from Cav. Cristoforo Negri to the Ministry's Secretary General, Turin 5 February 1863.

required people who spoke Chinese and were familiar with oriental culture, and so various scholars asked to be involved, including the engineer Sibaldi. He had studied in Edinburgh and London and had practised his profession in England, Egypt and the East Indies and in the service of their respective governments. His knowledge was mainly in the fields of ethnography and geography, and his presence was supposed to help with describing those far-off lands and assist in establishing consulates and other national representations.[6] The Ministry of the Navy, though recognizing the usefulness of a voyage to the Far East, both in the interests of trade and in instructing its crews, thought that the steamship "Regina" would be sufficient for its needs. As a matter of fact, the expenses for this campaign were too great to be met by the funds allocated by the budget for that financial year;[7] for this reason, the mission led by Mr. Negri never came to fruition. In 1866, Italy appointed an official with diplomatic experience to go to Shanghai, and from 1889, the consulate was managed by a consul whose function was more of an honorary than a technical or operational nature, which is surprising given Shanghai's strategic importance for international trade.

Following the bloody events that took place between the end of the nineteenth century and the beginning of the twentieth century in China, the idea began to take shape of strengthening Italy's representative offices to make them more than just honorary ones. Cesare Nerazzini was chosen as a second-class consul; he had served with the Colonial Office and knew Africa and Asia very well. He was convinced that Italy had to gradually find a way in among the other foreign powers and act above at political level, without trying to expand too much as this would risk compromising the geopolitical balances with the other powers. The ultimate goal was to emerge as a respected power within the limits imposed by a national economy that was still backward compared with the standards of the other European countries and the USA (Francioni 2004, 166).

Nerazzini's ideas made a significant contribution to Italy's presence and expansion in China, and they materialized in the establishment of an Italian trading house, which was supposed to make good use of the business of the Italian communities already present in China, carry out auxiliary tasks for the industrial and banking sectors and improve the direct shipping line between Italy and the Celestial Empire. As far as this last task was concerned, the national maritime services for the Far East envisaged a monthly voyage to Singapore, with the option of carrying on as far as Hong Kong. This service was inadequate for the needs of Italian trade, small though they were at that time, given that goods from Italy took fifty days on average to reach their destination, while the journey to Shanghai took almost three months, far longer than the direct international lines of other European shipping companies.

[6]Historical Diplomatic Archives of the Ministry of Foreign Affairs, Ministry of Foreign Affairs Writings: Kingdom of Italy 1861–1887, Busta 18, Fascicolo 7, Letter from the engineer Sibaldi to the Foreign Minister for the Kingdom of Italy, Florence 27 June 1863.

[7]Historical Diplomatic Archives of the Ministry of Foreign Affairs, Ministry of Foreign Affairs Writings: Kingdom of Italy 1861–1887, Busta 18, Fascicolo 7, Ministry of the Navy, Cabinet of the Minister, No. 1497, Subject: Mission in China, Turin, 17 May 1863.

The situation was such that Italian trade with Shanghai, both imports and exports, was actually in the hands of foreign operators, since Italy's entrepreneurs were at a disadvantage regarding travel times. Despite the continuous pressure exerted by Nerazzini, on both the government in Peking and the Italian government, the best that could be achieved was a grant to extend the existing Genoa-Singapore-Hong Kong line. Nerazzini must also be credited with having contributed to Italy's progress in China, thanks to the creation of a Chamber of Commerce. In 1902, the consul actually invited Italian entrepreneurs to organize a promotion committee, whose activities led to the creation of a Chamber of Commerce, which over time saw the number of its members increase from 30 in 1907, to 42 in 1910 and up to 128 in 1929.

The Chamber of Commerce worked in various ways: by publishing a regular bulletin, with economic and financial data above all for businessmen at home; creating procedures for friendly settlements of disputes between Italian and foreign entrepreneurs; and the dissemination ad advertising of Italian products suitable for export to China (Francioni 2004, 172–173). The protection of Catholic missionaries, as mentioned in the first chapter, was a useful means for making political inroads in China and setting up diplomatic representations. Thanks above all to the significant role played by the Vatican, this topic was strongly felt and widely debated in Italy at that time. From a numerical point of view, there were hundreds of Italians in China: nuns, missionaries (who came from the Franciscan seminaries of San Calogero in Milan and of Saints Peter and Paul in Rome) and priests grouped into eight papal vicariates located in the provinces of (Borsa 1961, 51):

(1) Shensi;
(2) Shansi;
(3) Shantung;
(4) Hunan;
(5) Henan;
(6) Eastern Hupeh;
(7) Western and southern Hupeh;
(8) Northern Hupeh.

A complex network of correspondence about the "missionary" question grew up between the end of 1880 and the start of 1890. Up until then, the old system was still in force, whereby French passports were given to missionaries regardless of their nationality, which was not mentioned in such passports. In a letter of 29 June 1887, the Royal Minister in Shanghai expressly asked for an end to this system and for the adoption of a new system, under which passports issued by the French Legation had to openly indicate the holder's nationality. Had this system not been adopted, France's unlawful monopoly over the missionaries would have become even further entrenched. For this reason, the Italian government sought the support of the Germans, convinced that, given the presence of a German papal vicariate in China, they would not allow French passports to be given to German subjects.[8]

[8]Historical Diplomatic Archives of the Ministry of Foreign Affairs, Ministry of Foreign Affairs Political Series Inventory A. 1888–1891, Busta 22, Fascicolo 7, *Protection in China of Italian*

The royal Italian government held that there was no legal basis for other powers to protect Italian subjects, since the latter had the right and the duty to be protected solely by the Italian State. The government referred to Article 9 of the treaty existing between Italy and China, which established that in the territory of the Celestial Empire, passports for Italian subjects could only be issued by the Italian authorities and then stamped only by the Chinese authorities.[9]

The Italian State also maintained that protection had to be not only individual, or rather limited to each individual missionary, but that it also had to be extended to their associations; it was also to be exercised without necessarily waiting for people to request it.[10] The response of Tsung-li Yamen at that time was that Italians holding passports issued by the Italian Legation enjoyed the same protection and the same privileges as French missionaries holding passports from the French Legation and that passports issued by other legations to Italian missionaries that did not show their nationality would not be stamped by the Chinese authorities.[11] This dispute continued over the years, with several differences of opinion between the Chinese authorities and those of the foreign countries involved. As we said before, there was a simple reason behind all this: the requests to protect their religious missionaries was very often a cover for their desire to penetrate China, to open legations and financial institutions, to exploit its raw materials and to bypass the procedures and limits set by the central government in Peking. This is one of the reasons why nowadays Christian missions are not particularly welcome in China, which does not recognize the Vatican's religious envoys and which has founded its own Catholic order which answers directly to the Communist Party of the People's Republic.[12]

Missionaries (1888–1890), Letter of the Royal Minister in Shanghai to the Ministry of Foreign Affairs, No. 1112, Subject: New phase of the dispute over French passports to missionaries in China, Shanghai, 29 June 1887.

[9]Historical Diplomatic Archives of the Ministry of Foreign Affairs, Ministry of Foreign Affairs Political Series Inventory A. 1888–1891, Busta 22, Fascicolo 7, *Protection in China of Italian Missionaries (1888–1890)*, directed memorandum from the Royal Legation in China to Tsung-li Yamen, Shanghai 5 June 1888.

[10]Historical Diplomatic Archives of the Ministry of Foreign Affairs, Ministry of Foreign Affairs Political Series Inventory A. 1888–1891, Busta 22, Fascicolo 7, *Protection in China of Italian Missionaries (1888–1890)*, Letter from Ferdinando De Luca to His Excellency the Minister of State for Foreign Affairs, n. general 71, report 43, Answer to letter April Div. 1Sez. 1, 10749/1b, Shanghai 5 June 1888.

[11]Historical Diplomatic Archives of the Ministry of Foreign Affairs, Ministry of Foreign Affairs Political Series Inventory A. 1888–1891, Busta 22, Fascicolo 7, *Protection in China of Italian Missionaries (1888–1890)*, Legation of His Majesty the King of Italy in China, general No. 179—report no. 116, Shanghai 31 October 1888.

[12]In 2018, a historic Vatican-China agreement was reached under Pope Francis in Peking; there had been no official relations between the two countries since 1949, when Mao Zedong proclaimed the People's Republic of China. The agreement does not conclude a process, but opens up new relations that will require constant negotiations between the Vatican and China.

4.3 Sino-Italian Treaties

The 1866 treaty with Italy officially established diplomatic and trade relations with China and was part of the Italian policy aimed at creating a commercial system based on free trade. Following the proclamation of the Kingdom of Italy, trade and navigation treaties had already been concluded with more than 17 countries, not only in Europe (Borsa 1961, 13). Furthermore, given the example of the other powers, Italy could not remain on the sidelines, and the main reason for this political decision was to preserve and expand its silk industry to take advantage of the rich and extensive Chinese market. On 29 September 1865, Luigi Torelli, Minister of Agriculture, sent King Victor Emmanuel II a report on the data from a survey on trade opportunities in China and stated that, in order to exploit the Chinese market from an economic point of view, an expedition was needed to formalize relations between the two countries. Torelli's suggestion convinced the King, Alfonso la Marmora, the Prime Minister, who was also responsible for Foreign Affairs, and Diego Angioletti, the Minister for the Navy, to set up a mission to sail to the coasts of China and Japan. The leader of the expedition was Admiral Vittorio Arminjon, who was given command of the steamship[13] "Magenta".

Arminjon was given full powers to draw up the treaty and to achieve three objectives: a political one, since it was the Magenta's first transatlantic voyage, it landed at several ports as it sailed along the coasts to bear witness to Italy's presence there, a diplomatic and trade one, given that the treaty with China was intended above all to expand trade for Italy's silk industry, and finally a scientific one, since this voyage was also meant to produce a report on nautical, ideological, morphological, zoological and botanical data and mementoes from the Far East to be used in Italy's museums (Francioni 2004, 19). As regards the drawing up of the treaty, the Admiral was asked to obtain the same privileges and rights already enjoyed by the other powers, above all in terms of trade regulations, customs tariffs and the right to open representations in the treaty ports. The Italian delegation's voyage began on 8 November 1865 when it left the port of Naples on board the steamship "Regina". On 2 February 1866, Arminjon arrived in Montevideo, Uruguay, where he transferred everyone onto the Magenta. Before reaching China, the Magenta landed in Japan, as Italy wanted to sign a treaty of amity with them too, which was duly signed on 25 August 1866 and which consisted of twenty-three articles: Italy managed to obtain the inclusion of a most favoured nation clause and the opening of the ports of Kanagawa, Nagasaki and Hakodate to trade with Italian subjects.

Having concluded business in Japan, Arminjon left for China, but he had to stop in Shanghai to get valid passports for himself and his men, as required by Chinese protocol, before they were allowed to travel to Peking and enter the city. It was very difficult to obtain safe conduct, but it was granted on 26 September 1865 and Arminjon's first act was to write a letter in which he announced his arrival in Peking as an envoy of the Italian king to all the consuls and ambassadors of the European

[13]The term steamship indicates a frigate that had both sails and a steam engine.

and North American powers, specifying that he had come to conclude a treaty of amity and trade with the Chinese Empire.

The letter was welcomed favourably by the Western diplomats, who gave their support and cooperation to the Italian captain, especially in writing a letter of introduction in order to begin talks with the Chinese authorities, which was done in the early days of October (Francioni 2004, 27–28).

It was thanks to the intervention of the European powers that the Italian expedition did not fail, as Prince Kung's initial response to the letter was negative, as he was convinced that Arminjon had obtained free entry into Peking in an irregular fashion, resorting to subterfuge and bribing the local officials.

Thanks to the explanations and the good offices of the Western diplomats, particularly those of the British Minister Sir Rutherford Alcock, the first official meeting took place on 14 October, at the headquarters of Tsung-li Yamen, between Vittorio Arminjon and the Chinese plenipotentiaries, namely T'an T'ing-hsiang, who was the first vice-president of the Ministry of Finance, and C'hung-hou, superintendent of the three ports and therefore delegated by the Emperor to negotiate with foreign powers. On 16 October, only two days after the negotiations, the Italian delegation presented its draft treaty containing fifty-three articles, which all translated into Chinese. In order to avoid any misunderstandings, Arminjon had stuck to a literal translation (sometimes copying entire articles) of the best parts of the treaties[14] that China had already concluded with other powers, so as to stop the Chinese from denying them any of the rights and prerogatives already granted to the other nations. One source of satisfaction for the Italians was obtaining the right to residence in Peking for an Italian diplomatic representative, while as far as the missionaries were concerned at that time, they were only able to achieve easier conditions for proselytization. One of the most sensitive points was setting a date for reviewing the treaty, especially the parts relating to the trade agreements and a possible revision of the customs tariffs: taking his cue from the Danish treaty, Arminjon asked for the treaty to be reviewed in 1868, but the Chinese objected, stating that the date was too close to when the treaty was to be concluded. Arminjon agreed on a review of the treaty after ten years, but took home a promise that the Chinese would sit round the negotiating table again should any other power request a treaty review before 1878 (Francioni s.d., 41–44). From the point of view of freedom to trade and tariffs, Italy obtained almost all of the concessions that had been granted to the other nations; instead, with regard to the most favoured nation clause, it was the Chinese delegates that insisted on the insertion of a clause, according to which "if any of the European Powers made any profitable concessions to China, which did not prejudice the interests of the Italian Government or Italian subjects, the Government of His Majesty the King would make every effort to adhere to it" (Francioni 2004, 32–33). This was in Article 54, paragraph 2, and was a "small diplomatic success" for the emissaries of the Emperor. The ceremonial signing of the treaty took place on 26 October 1866, with the seals affixed by T'han

[14]The treaties referred to were mainly those drawn up by France: the Treaty of Whampoa of 24 October 1844, that of Tientsin in 1858, and the Shanghai Agreement on customs tariffs and trade regulations concluded in 1858.

T'ing-hsiang and Vittorio Arminjon. The news of the positive outcome of the mission arrived in Italy by telegram on 23 November, and we can truly say that Italy's negotiator performed very well, achieving a result that satisfied Italy's expectations and a treaty that would constitute the basis of relations between Italy and China for a long time. Before analysing in detail the trade exchanges between Italy and China, we need to look ahead twenty years to a time when the idea of reviewing the 1866 Arminjon Treaty began to take hold.

In the two-year period 1902–1903, Great Britain, the USA, Japan and other nations demanded that new treaties be drawn up, because of the damage caused by the Boxer Rebellion and by the instability in China which had affected business for Western countries. Italy made its move somewhat later than the other countries, and negotiations were not opened with the Chinese government until 1905. Nevertheless, the possibility of reviewing the treaty had already sprung to mind as early as 1888, even though the Peking government never gave a positive answer to Italy's requests to that effect. The idea of reviewing the treaty was explicitly stated at the end of 1901, and Giulio Prinetti, Minister for Foreign Affairs, gave the consulate general in Shanghai the task of setting up an ad hoc commission that was supposed to formalize the text for a new trade treaty. Yet this commission was never effectively operational, and the project was never implemented. After the foreign powers had drawn up new treaties in 1902 and 1903, Italy could no longer remain on the sidelines. It was only in 1905 that the Minister for Foreign Affairs, Tommaso Tittoni, ordered Giovanni Gallina and Consul Nerazzini to prepare a document on the state of Italy's interests in China, which could then be used as a memorandum for the ministers responsible for the diplomatic preparations for concluding a new treaty.

Gallina and Nerazzini drew up a very realistic and rather unedifying document about Italy's interests in China: the two writers deliberately neglected the trade aspects (Torelli, who was the Minister of Agriculture, had drawn up a report to that effect; see above) and aimed at strengthening the political element, asserting that Italy could not be content with a defeatist policy in the Far East, as this would mean being far too subordinate compared with the other countries. The points they discussed most were a greater insistence on protecting the missionaries and, from a trade point of view, a concerted effort to make the Chinese hire specialized Italians in the silk industry as well as to open new ports to Italian ships, as envisaged in the new treaties concluded with the other nations. As regards the central topic that had characterized the negotiations between China and the treaty powers, namely the abolition of the *likin* in exchange for an increase in the import tariffs, Italy, whose few goods were destined for the above-mentioned new ports, had no reason to endorse this initiative since there was no material advantage involved (Francioni 2004, 194–196). However, the Italian government's policy diverged from the analyses made by Gallina and Nerazzini.

In a letter sent by Tittoni to Carlo Baroli, the Italian representative in Peking, the Minister supported the idea of keeping a low profile in China, with no further territorial ambitions (Italy had already obtained the concession of Tientsin), in order to maintain more friendly relations with China compared with other countries, and thus make it easier to increase private commercial and industrial business.[15] Here, we can clearly see the differences in opinion between Rome and the Italian delegation in Peking. The instructions given by the Italian government to Nerazzini were therefore to draw up an agreement based on the Anglo-Chinese treaty of 1902, while the proposals made in the Gallina-Nerazzini report were essentially rejected. Nerazzini declared himself unwilling to support a defeatist policy for Italy in China that only sought to obtain the bare minimum. In contrast, the consul took a longer-term view and pushed for strong political decisions, such as the "no ifs and no buts" protection of the missionaries and the establishment of four career consular officials together with a greater commitment to the claim on the province of Chekiang. As regards the *likin*, the government believed it was better not to oppose its abolition, unlike Nerazzini.

At the beginning of June, the commission comprising Nerazzini, Gravina and Riva drew up the final draft treaty, which consisted of twelve articles, five of which were new while the others transposed the agreements already signed by China with the other foreign powers. Articles 1–4 referred to trade: they asked for the ports of Wushi and Shaoxing to be opened to foreign traffic, the establishment of schools of sericulture to improve the quality of cocoons, and the safeguarding of Italian-owned spinning mills and of all the Italians working in the trade sector. Article 5 was the most important one in the draft, because if the clause was accepted "it would ensure preferential rights for Italy on the concessions that the Chinese government made to foreign businessmen in Chekiang and Hsi-shan for activities in the mining and railway sectors" (Francioni 2004, 208). The other points in the draft treaty incorporated the requests in the previous treaties concluded by China with the USA and Great Britain, in relation to steam navigation on the inland waterways, the reform of the judicial system and the rights connected with extraterritoriality.

The draft did not therefore follow the guidelines laid down by the government; it was far more ambitious; Nerazzini decided to inform the government about this differing line of action and intended to stand firm: however, there was a series of governmental crises and nobody officially countered Nerazzini's intentions. He maintained his line of conduct and was prepared to present his project to the delegates of the Peking government. By the end of June, the articles had been translated into Chinese and were then shown to the emissaries of the imperial government, Lu haihuan, Sheng-hsuan-hai and Li Ching-Fang, who was a member of the commission for reviewing the tariffs. The most difficult part of the dialogue was presenting the clause in Article 5 to the Chinese. The problem was that this clause, which guaranteed a significant advantage for Italy's interests, had to be introduced extremely carefully, given the rivalry that could arise with the other nations and particularly because two of the members of the tariff review committee were British citizens, Hippisley and Taylor, who might have tried to stonewall it. For this reason the Italian delegation submitted the text of Article 5 to Lu privately, which made it take on the semblance of a secret clause. The request took Lu by surprise, although after

[15]Historical Diplomatic Archives of the Ministry of Foreign Affairs, Political Series Inventory A, 1888–1891, Letter from the Foreign Minister Tittoni to Carlo Baroli, Rome 16 January 1905.

discussing it with his superiors, he did not veto it. On 26 July, the treaty, comprising eleven articles, was presented in a public session and apart from a few grievances aired by the British, everything went very smoothly as far as the Western commissioners were concerned. However, as regards some articles presented by Nerazzini that were different compared with those of previous treaties, the Chinese plenipotentiaries declared that they would be forced to ask the viceroy's plenipotentiaries for an opinion, thereby postponing the final phase of the negotiations.

The ensuing pause was fortuitous, since it meant there was time to resolve some misunderstandings between the parties owing to some translation mistakes, which were swiftly corrected. Nerazzini then presented the final version of the text, from which the clause in Article 5 was missing, which was going to be discussed separately and confidentially by the plenipotentiaries of the two governments. Lu hai-huan, having spoken with his superiors, let it be understood that the government would have no difficulty in approving the clause. Yet on 21 August, the Shanghai newspaper "Nan-fang-pao" published the news that the Chinese Ministry of Trade had decided to award the contract for building a railway line from Peking to Mento-kuo in the Hsi-shan Province to a French company. The news infuriated the Italian delegation, as it was a violation of the previous agreements. After a series of meetings, at the end of September the Chinese delegation informed the Italians that it was willing to sign a treaty similar to those concluded with the other powers, including the abolition of the *likin* and an increase in the import tariffs, but that it was not disposed to accept the clause included in Article 5. Nerazzini insisted on this point for several days, but it was systematically opposed by the Chinese, and the consul was increasingly convinced that the debate over Article 5 was an excuse to make changes to some of the other articles too. Given the situation, Nerazzini wrote a letter on 6 October, translated by Vitale and read out in one of the meetings, in which he took note of China's decisions, and by virtue of the full powers granted to him, he broke off negotiations that same day.

This took the imperial delegates by surprise, since in this way the Chinese would not obtain the clause that was most important to them, namely the abolition of the *likin* and the increase in the tariffs. With the help of Western diplomats, the two delegations tried to find joint solutions, but Nerazzini realized that any attempt to protect Italy's interests clashed with China's policy, which was to gradually eliminate all the requests it disliked. Given the situation, on 25 October the Italian consul left a letter with the commission in which it accused the imperial government of refusing all of Italy's requests and in this way officially announced the end of the negotiations to review the treaty. This letter effectively brought the negotiations to a close and created a precedent, since other countries such as France, Belgium and the Netherlands understood that it would be useless to start any treaty negotiations since they would not obtain any more than Great Britain, Japan and the USA had. The most favoured nation clause meant they had all the advantages guaranteed for foreigners without having to agree on abolishing the *likin* (Francioni 2004, 216–226). While it did not create economic disadvantages in the short term, this breakdown in negotiations damaged diplomatic relations between Italy and China and had consequences for the following twenty years. As will be seen in Chap. 3, only with the advent of Fascism would Italy become important again in China, both politically and commercially.

Chapter 5
Trade and Commerce

Abstract This chapter offers an historical economic analysis of Italy's international trade relations: in particular, the worsening of trade relations with France that started in 1888 was one of the reasons for the gravity of the crisis that manifested itself in the following years and that was suffered above all in southern Italy. In the long run, however, it had the positive effect of increasing the multilaterality of Italy's international relationships, including that with China. Italian foreign trade appears positive during this period (1861–1919). As reported by Zamagni (Dalla periferia al centro. La seconda rinascita economica dell'Italia 1861–1981. Il Mulino, Bologna, p. 156, 1990) between the years 1866–68 and 1913 the annual growth rate of imports was 3.1% and that of exports 2.7%. However, Italy's share of world trade fell (from 3.1 to 2.6%) as it failed to keep pace with the expansion of international trade in other countries (Federico in Meridiana 4:163–196, 1988). As regards exports, those of raw materials (sulphur and metallic minerals) and traditional agricultural products (oil, wine, eggs and rice) declined. Only raw hemp and rawhides registered an increase in the category of unprocessed products. This result was certainly due to the process of industrialization initiated in the 1880–1913 period which, on the one hand, had transformed the productive sectors and, on the other, had expanded the internal demand for raw materials and foodstuffs. The scenario changed after 1923. One of the main features of this change was the more marked territorial diversification of Italian foreign trade which, while it gives a glimpse of German predominance, does not recreate the dependence of Italian trade on a single country that existed in the period up to 1887 (year of the agrarian crisis and of the law of 14 July 1887 imposing the agrarian tariff with a distinctly protectionist power (Toniolo, in Storia economica dell'Italia liberale 1850–1918. Il Mulino, Bologna, 1988) which led to the break with France).

5.1 Trade Relations

With the Arminjon treaty, the Italian government had laid the foundations for long-lasting diplomatic and trade relations with China, in order to open its market to this Far Eastern country and to find new outlets for its products.

D. Strangio, *Italy-China Trade Relations*, Studies in Economic History,
https://doi.org/10.1007/978-3-030-39084-6_5

Italy had no intention of meddling in China's domestic affairs, and neither did it want to be involved in the dispute between China and the other Western countries. With regard to this, the Italian representative, the first of whom was Count Sallier de la Tour, chose not to reside in Peking, which was the diplomatic centre and the capital; he opted for Shanghai instead, where a consulate general was opened, as it was one of the most important trading centres in the whole of China (Borsa 1961, 35). Up until 1865, trade exchanges between China and Italy had been minimal. As Vittorio Arminjon wrote:

> ...Italy could offer no cotton fabrics, or metals or any of the goods most frequently sought after in the Chinese ports: it uses very little tea and makes more silk than it needs.... (Mancini 1987, 418)

Nevertheless, Luigi Torelli, Minister of Agriculture, was convinced that the opening of the Suez Canal would mean significant improvements for Italy's economy which was struggling at that time, and so he had a series of analyses and studies carried out on what the best items for Italy to export to China could be. It would have been advantageous to export mercury, gold and silver thread, textiles, glassware, knives, soap and weapons to China; Italian wine companies could have gained a market share, but they had to compete with Spain and Portugal. There was little room for primary goods such as olive oil, pulses, and fruit and vegetables, since demand was almost entirely met by the local economy (Mancini 1987, 422). Despite this, however, from the conclusion of the contract to the end of the nineteenth century, trade relations never took off between Italy and China. Table 5.1 exemplifies this trend.

The number of Italian residents in the open ports increased over the years, but their numbers remained low compared with other foreigners; ships flying the Italian flag were rarely seen, and they generally tended to sail to the port of Hong Kong (which was not officially Chinese territory at that time) and any ships that did come were of small tonnage and only arrived occasionally since there were no regular shipping lines.

These statistical data only give an approximate indication of the situation, as a certain amount of Italian goods entered China through English and German companies, and entered Italy indirectly above all through France. The goods transported by Italian ships to Chinese ports were of very modest value: in 1872, the value of

Table 5.1 Italians and Italian trade contracts (1872–1891)

Years	1872	1875	1876	1883	1884	1891
Italians living in open ports	23	25	28	123	129	133
Italian commercial enterprises	2	2	2	3	3	4
Movement under the Italian flag in Chinese ports (arrivals and departures)	4	4	2	4	nn.	8

Source The data in the table are from reports by the consuls in China, published in the *Bollettino Consolare* (Consular Bulletin): vol. XI, p. 181 (for 1872), vol. XI P. II, p. 105 (1875); vol. XIII P. II, p. 537 (1876); vol. XXI P. II, p. 157 (1883–1884); 1895 P. II, p. 47 (1891)

the goods exported stood at 45,016 lire, while that of goods imported was 9952 lire. These figures are negligible, if we consider that British ships carried goods worth 519,101,912 lire in terms of exports and 358,956,824 lire for imports (Borsa 1961, 36). However, there are not enough trade data available to define the situation in terms of the assets and liabilities on Italy's trade balance, in the years following the Arminjon treaty and up until the last decade of the nineteenth century. Since from 1888 onwards and even during the best years of the first decade of the Mussolini government, Italy's trade balance was constantly negative, it can be presumed that in the period in question the level of Italy's exports must have been very low. Italy, like other countries, took part in the trafficking of opium, which was legally permitted by the 1858 Anglo-Chinese treaty.

Although cultivated relatively little in Italy, opium could be sold to farmers and merchants that sold large batches of it in the ports of the Mediterranean basin, earning sums that ranged from 55 to 65 francs per kilogram, given the high levels of opium consumption in China, especially in intellectual and noble circles (Mancini 1987, 419). Furthermore, another significant form of trafficking was the transport of coolies. They were unskilled workers, often forcibly recruited and who were transported to the big islands in Oceania, to Latin America, California and to Panama to dig the Canal. They were kept in dreadful conditions, especially during sea voyages, where they were shut in the hold with very little food. They were subjected to a regime of forced labour with no protection and the coolie trade increased considerably after the abolition of slavery in the USA thanks to President Abraham Lincoln.

The nerve centre for enrolling these coolies was Macao, an island controlled by the Portuguese who were tolerant of this traffic. Slaves were actually recruited here, especially hungry peasants from the countryside who were sent to the Chinese ports and shipped off to the various parts of the world where they were needed. Of the roughly 13,000 coolies who left from Macao, more than 6000 were carried by ships flying the Italian flag (Borsa 1961, 20). From a numerical point of view, a total of 106,000 coolies left Macao for Cuba and Lima in the decade 1858–1868. With the conclusion of the treaty of 1866, and therefore with the start of regular diplomatic relations, this traffic could no longer be tolerated, all the more so because in 1865 France and Great Britain had drawn up an agreement with the Chinese government on the question of coolies. Between the end of the nineteenth century and the beginning of the twentieth century, trade exchanges between Italy and China recorded a modest increase, though nowhere near the growth rates of the other Western countries. This progress was made thanks to the work of the Italian diplomatic delegation in Peking (especially on the part of Nerazzini), which used communications, telegrams and letters to urge the Italian government to exploit more fully the vast territory of China, largely unknown to Italians.

Many people tended to judge China by what they could see in the open ports, where foreigners were predominant and had, to a certain extent, modified the customs and habits of the native people there. It was also true that outside of the most important cities, China remained as it had been under the Ming dynasty, with the difference that, while in those days the existence of foreigners was unknown, in the nineteenth century foreigners were hated and despised because of their colonialist approach.[1] Yet aside from the various open ports (the port of Chong-Qing was opened in 1890, a city located on the Yangtze river, 300 miles from the port of Yichang, and its construction was followed by Italian diplomats so that they could exploit that area for their trade),[2] there were huge areas of China that had never had any contact with foreigners and that could be a useful source for imports and exports.

These are the reasons that pushed Italian diplomats to go to Peking and ask for greater Italian political and trade involvement in Chinese affairs. As far as imports are concerned, in the last decade of the nineteenth century, raw silk was by far the most important.

In 1892, imported silk amounted to an annual average of 2500 bales, which rose to 4821 in 1893, 4858 in 1894 and reached a total of almost 9000 in 1895. This sharp increase in the space of just a few years was also due to the fact that Milan was the main European market for silk, having overtaken Lyon and London. The next item down on the list of imports was hides, especially bovine ones, followed by cotton and sesame seeds (Borsa 1961, 36). The share of exports, albeit larger than in the 1860s and 70s, was negligible since it was difficult for Italian ships to satisfy the demand for goods such as opium, processed metals, cotton and tea. In the late 1880s, there was a steady decline in the export of tea which, together with silk was the most important item in the Empire's total exports, and this decrease was a serious threat to the prospects for international trade.

The difficulties stemmed from the strong competition from India, due to the very high quality of the goods produced there. The decrease was so marked that the imperial government itself began to be concerned, but there is no particular evidence of any worries on the Italian side, given that Italy was absolutely not an exporter of tea.[3] However, among the products exported there was a marginal amount of cotton, silk, coral, wines, processed marble, hats and hides. In 1887 the direct export of buffalo hides to the port of Shanghai totalled around 1105 bales and weighed 89,700 kg, mostly from the port of Genoa.[4] In the space of two years, in 1889 the amount of hides rose by roughly 7000 kg, leading to a total of 96,500 kg of exported hides, mainly leaving from the port of Livorno, followed by Venice, Naples,

[1]Historical Diplomatic Archives of the Ministry of Foreign Affairs, Political Series Inventory. A 1888–1891, Busta 22—Fascicolo 7, Legation of H.M. the King of Italy in China, Letter from the Prince of Cariati, Peking 16 December 1889.

[2]Historical Diplomatic Archives of the Ministry of Foreign Affairs, Political Series Inventory. A 1888–1891, Busta 22—Fascicolo 7, Legation of H.M. the King of Italy in China, Peking 25 August 1890.

[3]Historical Diplomatic Archives of the Ministry of Foreign Affairs, Political Series Inventory. A 1888–1891, Busta 22—Fascicolo 7, Legation of H.M. the King of Italy in China, Peking 10 March 1890.

[4]Historical Diplomatic Archives of the Ministry of Foreign Affairs, Political Series Inventory. A 1888–1891, Busta 22—Fascicolo 7, Legation of H.M. the King of Italy in Shanghai, Shanghai 8 November 1889.

Ancona, Messina and Palermo.[5] A product that caught the attention of the Italian representatives and could have become a source of wealth for the (few) companies operating in China was mineral water, which could have replaced ordinary tap water and been an important source of trade in all China's ports, where there was little or no drinking water available, since it was obtained by filtering water from the rivers.

Up until that time and in contrast with countries such as Germany, despite being rich in mineral resources, Italy had not managed to organize any appreciable exports. It now began to introduce mineral water in a methodical way, imitating the bottles and labels of "Apollinaris", one of the most widespread German mineral waters. In addition, this kind of product was exempt from any kind of customs duty in China, and storage costs and fees never exceeded 10% of the value of the goods.[6] Despite Italy's good intentions, however, mineral water never became a significant item on the list of Italy's exports to China. In short, therefore, despite a small increase compared with the post-unification years, the level of imports and exports to and from China was extremely modest in the last years of the nineteenth century, than the other occidental countries (expecially Germany).

The situation altered very little up until 1920, also because in the early years of the twentieth century, diplomatic relations between Italy and China hardened, with unavoidable consequences for Italy's trade balance under the heading "China". These years were characterized by an internal power struggle in China between conservatives and reformists, which led to the outbreak of civil war and eventually to the proclamation of the first Chinese Republic in 1911, but the war continued to creep on through the years, becoming a bloodbath in the period 1930–1950. In those years, there was also strong competition between the European countries to provide war supplies, both legally and secretly, to the warring parties.

The central government in Peking, which was paying out huge sums, at least three times higher than normal prices, had to turn to Europe to buy considerable amounts of munitions: the rebels found things more difficult, as they had had to face great expense in purchasing rifles and guns in order to arm all the insurgents rushing from all over China to increase the numbers of revolutionary troops. Italy did not stand idle, and various letters and telegrams arrived from China with the aim of making Rome aware of the need to exploit the situation. The first step was to try and sell the revolutionary troops about 1,500,000 Vetterli-Vitali[7] rifles that had been allocated to the Ministry of War and which had to be disposed of because they were obsolete. The Royal Legation in China could not deal with or expose itself in this affair, given that the weapons in question were to be sold to those opposing the government: for this reason, it was decided to place the order for this business with the Coloni &

[5]Historical Diplomatic Archives of the Ministry of Foreign Affairs, Political Series Inventory. A 1888–1891, Busta 22—Fascicolo 7, Legation of H.M. the King of Italy in Shanghai, Shanghai 28 December 1890.

[6]Historical Diplomatic Archives of the Ministry of Foreign Affairs, Political Series Inventory. A 1888–1891, Busta 22—Fascicolo 7, Letter from the Regent of the Consulate Ernesto Ghisi, Subject: experiment to export mineral water from Italy, Shanghai 11 September 1890.

[7]The Vetterli-Vitali Mod. 1870/87 was a revolving-sliding shutter rifle supplied to the armed forces of the Kingdom of Italy.

Co. company in Shanghai, which held a "Borsa di Pratica Commerciale all'Estero" (Foreign Trade Exchange). Three objectives could be achieved in this way: an Italian company was given the business, the profit margin was good and the Ministry of War could finally dispose of rifles that were worth nothing to Italy.[8]

The Italian government acted prudently, because if even a small indiscretion had come out about the sale of weapons during a civil war, it could have led to foreigners being persecuted and massacred; it endorsed the project presented, but it asked for the Minister of War to be considered as completely unconnected with the sale of the Vetterli-Vitali. It was too good an opportunity to miss, since the reigning anarchy and provincial decentralization would later increase the demand for armaments in every province.[9] As well as small arms, Italy was also interested in supplying China with warships. In 1912, the Chinese government decided to set up a Ministry for the Navy and to assemble a small fleet of warships. The funds required would be amassed by collecting a predetermined sum from each province and by putting a tax on rail tickets. A letter was sent from Peking on 30 December 1907 to urge the Italian government to act by informing Italian shipbuilders who wanted to be involved in the project, since the Chinese government intended to purchase ten or so warships from Germany. The Chinese Minister was accordingly invited to Rome so that he could visit some of Italy's shipyards and ships and be given all the information he might need, refer everything to the authorities in Peking and propose working with Italy's shipbuilding sector.[10] In the following spring the Peking government calculated that about 15 million taels (50 million francs) were needed to finance the overhauling of its navy. Four cruisers and forty torpedo boats were going to be ordered, so as to put together a fleet of one hundred ships.[11] Owing to a lack of statistical data and official documents, we do not know whether Italy actually managed to sell these warships to China at that time, but what we can say is that both the Italian Legation in Peking and the Italian government were keenly interested in an arms trade with China.

It can be concluded that, if the level of imports and exports in out of China was not terribly impressive at that time, Italy had a strong but hardly commendable interest in trafficking opium, coolies and weapons. There were several factors contributing to the modest relations between Italy and China in the sixty years between unification and the advent of the Fascist regime. First and foremost was Italy's total ignorance

[8]Historical Diplomatic Archives of the Ministry of Foreign Affairs, Political Series P. 1891–1916, Pacco 422, Posizione 86/3 *Arms sales in China*, Letter from Dr. Eugenio Donegani to His Excellency Mr. Nitti, The Minister of Agriculture, Industry and Commerce, Peking 7 November 1911.

[9]Historical Diplomatic Archives of the Ministry of Foreign Affairs, Political Series P 1891–1916, Letter from His Excellency the Marquis of San Giuliano to Count Sforza, No. 747/207, Subject: possible sale of Italian sales.

[10]Historical Diplomatic Archives of the Ministry of Foreign Affairs, Political Series P 1891–1916, Pacco 511, *Purchase and construction of warships*, Legation of H.M. the King of Italy in China, No. 833/249, Letter from Livio Borghese to His Excellency Senator T. Tittoni, the Minister for Foreign Affairs, Peking 30 December 1907.

[11]Historical Diplomatic Archives of the Ministry of Foreign Affairs, Political Series Inventory P 1891–1916, Pacco 511, *Purchase and construction of warships*, Legation of H.M. the King of Italy in China, No. 74/18, Letter from Livio Borghese to His Excellency Senator T. Tittoni, the Minister of Foreign Affairs, Peking 25 January 1908.

regarding the Chinese market, and Chinese life and culture: Italians thought that China was a barbarian country, closed to trade with the west, but they also judged it by the same yardstick as they would a European country, and were under the illusion that they could trade with China using European systems.

This was not true, as Arminjon recalled in his memoirs, since the Chinese market was subject to certain singularities (Borsa 1961, 38). European and American merchants could only reside within the consular jurisdiction of the open ports, yet trade could only take place with people living in the hinterland. It was therefore necessary first of all to be permanently resident there and work towards having as many consulates and diplomatic representations opened as possible. In 1889 there were only nine Italian trading houses in China and 124 residents, against 402 British trading houses and 5600 residents (Germany and France also had numerous residents compared with Italy). There were only two ships flying the Italian flag in the Chinese ports and they carried very little merchandise in relation to the Empire's total volume of traffic. Another reason which held back the development of fruitful trade relations for many years was the lack of a "fast" and direct shipping line from Italy to China, to make it quicker to transport both goods and people. Yet the main reason for the scarce progress in Italy's trade with China was the inadequacy of its diplomatic and consular representation. Up until 1889, the consulate in Shanghai was represented by honorary consuls, who were also mostly foreigners.

In that same year in order to place the Italian representatives in more direct contact with the Chinese authorities and to have more information to send to the Italian ministries,[12] the legation was transferred to Peking and a second-class person was appointed to Shanghai (Borsa 1961, 41). The reports sent by Italian diplomats were generalized and not very up to date and provided very little information to help Italian traders overcome the difficulties of the Chinese market. When the legation was moved to Peking, it was governed by the Prince of Cariati, who had only been in China for a year and knew almost nothing about it.

Alberto Pansa was the first Italian representative to live in Peking, and he tried to reorganize the diplomatic representation by using instruments and ceremonies that were of great social importance in China, but the modest funds at his disposal made this almost impossible (Borsa 1961, 45). The better organization and greater involvement of Italian diplomacy were due to Consul Nerazzini, who as we said worked hard to try and increase Italy's political and commercial presence in China, despite being hindered by vetoes from the government in Rome, which showed little interest in that far-off land and was caught up in the continual squabbles and plotting of Italian politics.

[12]Historical Diplomatic Archives of the Ministry of Foreign Affairs, Political Series Inventory A 1888–1891, Extract from a letter of the Prince of Cariati, Shanghai, 10 June 1888.

5.2 San Mun Bay (Sān Mén Xiàn): The Idea of an "Italian" Territory in China

The 1894–95 war between China and Japan marked the beginning of a new era in the relations between China and the other powers. Starting from 1898, they asked to rent territories and to acquire concessions, such as the bay of Kiao-ciau for Germany, the peninsula of Liaotung for the Russians and the bay of Kwang-chow for the French. Italy could not remain indifferent to such events, and discussions began and opinions were formed in Italy at both parliamentary level and among the general public. On 16 February, the undersecretary Lelio Bonin Longare declared that the King's Government would be wary of any adventurous policy that might create dangers and disappointments for Italy, but would continue to promote and increase Italy's trade in the Far East (Borsa 1961, 75).

The Minister for Foreign Affairs, Visconti Venosta, adopted a bolder stance and believed that in order to consolidate its political and commercial interests, Italy would have to engage in direct action similar to that of the other powers.

To this end, the government sent a warship, the *Marco Polo*, to the Far East in order to guard and protect Italian interests. It also sent one of its best Italian diplomats, the *Commendatore* (Knight Commander) Renato De Martino and studied various forms of funding to enhance consular activity; it also pushed Italian industrial representatives to set up trade missions in China in order to understand the potential of the Chinese market for Italian exports.

Yet Visconti Venosta did not stop here; he was aware of Italy's weak position in China compared with the other powers and began to consider the idea of occupying a coastal location. The minister appointed the Marquis Salvago Raggi, chargé d'affaires in Peking, to write a report on the possibility of occupying a direct port of call in China. He wondered above all what the Chinese reaction might be, what the best area for Italy to request was and what the diplomatic responses were likely to be to Italy's request (Borsa 1961, 77). The government had not indicated any particular location or any specific interest to be safeguarded; in addition, neither Raggi nor his team had any broad economic, political or geographical knowledge of China.

The report delivered by Raggi, and drafted in the field by Naval Commander Incoronato, suggested occupying the port of Samsa instead of that of San Mun (Sān Mén Xiàn), which would require huge sums of money. Fearing that the other powers would refuse Italy's request, the smallest bay was chosen, that of San Mun, which opened onto the populous and wealthy region of Chekiang: it was about a third of the size of Italy and had 12 million inhabitants (Coco 2017a; b, 185–214). It had not been occupied by other foreign powers because it would be very difficult to make it into a maritime and trade centre, since the bay was a long way from the main communication routes and a long way from the large economic hubs such as Canton and Shanghai.

In the early months of 1899, the news of Italy's request for San Mun appeared in several newspapers; Japan, USA and Germany initially adopted a stance of benevolent neutrality. The German government was the first to be informed about the

Italian plan; Germany was Italy's best ally in China and the German ministers had already cooperated with the Italian ones over the issue of protecting the Catholic missionaries. Germany therefore gave its approval to the Italian request, stating that it would not obstruct Italy, but it could not give support publicly so as not to damage its relationship with the Chinese Empire. The Japanese on the other hand gave their immediate and unreserved support. Japan was sympathetic to Italy's request because it would ensure a safe "neighbour" close to the island of Formosa and give Japan the chance to increase its influence in that area. The US government's stance was neutral but in accordance with the general principles of American policy.

The USA supported the Italian project, although like Germany, they did not give their approval to Italy's request for diplomatic support from the Chinese government (Borsa 1961, 92–95; 1969). It seemed that the only difficulties might be caused by Great Britain, since Chekiang, the province that Italy wanted to control, bordered on the Yangtze valley and the Chusan Islands; the British and the Peking government had agreed not to dispose of them. However, there were no particular disagreements between Rome and London, and Italy was certainly not a power that could weaken British interests in China.

However, Great Britain asked Italy for assurances that its territorial and political influence would not extend beyond San Mun to other areas, and gave its consent to the project on the understanding that if Italy used any force there, Britain would intervene against Italian interests, since any use of force would destabilize British policy aimed at keeping the peace in the Far East, a prerequisite for protecting their industrial and trade interests. Having given the necessary assurances and obtained British support too, Italy prepared to draft a formal request to the Chinese government for the occupation of the bay.

Apart from Austria, which declared that this was an act of violence on the part of Italy, the only power that opposed Italy's request was Russia, who saw it as a way to indirectly help Great Britain with its anti-Russian plans in the Far East. On 26 February 1899, Italy's representatives in China were instructed by Rome to forward the request concerning the renting of San Mun bay and the recognition of Italian interests in the province of Chekiang to the Chinese authorities. Yet only a few days after the "positive" reactions of the foreign powers (aside from Russia), in March 1899, the Chinese refused to grant the concession:[13] the main reason for this was that China wanted to maintain friendly relations with Italy, which would inevitably have been marred if the Italian operation had been successful. This refusal was also a test of strength for the Chinese Empire, which for the first time felt that it could oppose a foreign power without resorting to violence.

The Italian chargé d'affaires in China, surprised by the Chinese refusal to negotiate, sent a telegram to the Chinese government with an ultimatum for the occupation of San Mun; however, following advice from the British diplomats, he realized that he had acted somewhat hastily and rashly, and so he sent a second telegram in which

[13]Historical Diplomatic Archives of the Ministry of Foreign Affairs Political Series Inventory P 1891–1916, Letter by His Excellency the Hon. Grinetti from the Royal legation in Tokyo, Subject: rumours of new paperwork for the concessions of San Mun, Tokyo 24 April 1902.

he invited the Chinese government to disregard the indications contained in the first telegram. However, unluckily for Italy, the second telegram arrived before the first one, to the great annoyance of the Chinese who replied with a second refusal and expressed their indignation over Italy's ultimatum (see Coco 2019, 328–349).

This was a severe blow to Italy's prestige in the Far East, which would have consequences over the following decades up until the advent of Fascism; furthermore, this failure also caused non-material damage to the other powers who already held a section of coastline and material damage to those who were trying to acquire one, since the Italian situation had given the Chinese government the strength and courage to reject other foreign proposals. Nevertheless, in the space of a few years, Italy managed to obtain a concession in the area of Tientsin, which was not very prosperous and therefore unimportant for the other powers (Mondaini 1927, 243).

5.3 The Concession of Tientsin (Tianjin)

Despite the poor figure cut by Italy in the San Mun affair, it was not long before Italy managed to obtain a concession from China that equalled those made to the other powers: to fully understand the importance of this matter, we need to take a step back and examine the Boxer Rebellion.

In April 1900, the Boxers attacked the first Catholic missions in the country and, on their way to Peking, they also attacked villages, damaging telegraph and railway networks, and soon struck against the foreign representations. Following requests for help from the Chinese government, the foreign powers could not stand by and do nothing; they sent an international military expedition of soldiers from various countries to put down the rebellion. Italy also played a part in this, sending soldiers and warships. Taking part in this international expedition after thirty years of relations with China gave Italy the opportunity to redeem its lack of commitment and inconclusive attempts to make headway there, as well as its insignificant economic interests compared with those of the other countries "occupying" Chinese land (Francioni 2004, 143; Corradini 1991b).

Italy intervened in the war operations with over 2400 men, including officers and foot soldiers, supported by six units of the blue-water navy. The Minister for Foreign Affairs, Visconti Venosta, sent a telegram to Admiral Candiani, advising him that "from a political point of view it was desirable for at least some of our troops to head to Peking, as it was important for an Italian contingent to be part of the international occupation in Peking" (Mondaini 1927, 246). After normality had been restored and the Boxer Rebellion suppressed, Italy, like the other powers and in order to re-establish normal diplomatic relations with Peking, asked China to punish the leaders of the rebellion severely, as well as for adequate compensation for the unrest and inconveniences suffered by the international community in China.

This was a chance to obtain territorial concessions and financial compensation, and so both the Italian government and its representative in Peking, Salvago Raggi, played a considerable part in the discussions on the payment of indemnities and on the loans made in relation to the Boxer affair.

However, these objectives clashed with the agreement that regulated the international expedition, which was considered to be an international policing operation to re-establish the status quo, with the preserving of China's territorial integrity and the "Open Door" principle. Every country had been party to this agreement, except for Russia, which wanted to complete its hegemony over the territory of Manchuria. However, the government was united on this front: on one side, there were those who wanted to stay within the limits of the international agreement: the objective was to receive payment for the expenses incurred by the Royal Italian government and for the damage caused to Italian citizens, so as to reinstate good relations with the other powers and with China; on the other side, there was Minister Visconti Venosta, who wanted to take advantage of the opportunity to consolidate Italian assets in China, and gave Admiral Candiani the task of exploring places and territories suitable for Italian occupation. The Admiral and his team had found an ideal location in the Gulf of Nimrod to request as a concession, since it was near the province of Chekiang, one of the most important silk-producing areas: the objective shared by the Admiral and the Minister for Foreign affairs was, however, blocked by the explicit disinterest of the Rome government, which did not want to develop or support initiatives that might clash with the political stance maintained by Italy up until then throughout the Far East.

On 20 November 1900, the Rome government received the news that "the Russians and the Belgians had occupied useable areas near Tientsin, of around four square kilometres and half a square kilometre respectively, and that the Austro-Hungarian Minister had sent a telegram to his government asking permission to reserve equal rights for Austro-Hungarian subjects" (Mondaini 1927, 246). Italy saw this as an opportunity to be seized, and on 19 January 1901 the Italian Minister in Peking, acting on a request of some Italian citizens who wanted to manufacture and open businesses in Tientsin, asked for the authorization to temporarily occupy some land that had not yet been occupied by the Russians, and asked the Chinese government to regularize the granting of the area at a later date.

The Chinese government had recognized the occupation of some neighbouring areas by the German government and could not therefore refuse a similar authorization for Italy, whose actions in China were also supported by the new Foreign Minister, the Honourable Giulio Prinetti. He asked for formal steps to be taken and for clear requests to be made to the Chinese government to avoid a "second San Mun".

The occupation of the neighbouring areas was entrusted to Lieutenant Mario Valli, who completed operations by occupying an area located between the Russian and Austrian concessions on 21 January 1901, between the Chinese suburb of Yu chia-chang and the railway line to Peking. It was only on 7 June 1902 that the de facto occupation became official, thanks to the agreement concluded by Count

Gallina, sent by His Majesty the King of Italy to China, with Tang-shao-I, who was in charge of China's maritime customs. The instrument used was that of the concession, with no time limits or financial burdens, except for the payment of an annual rent (Francioni 2004, 149–150). The document that formalized the concession contained 14 articles, which defined the boundaries and laid down that the property of the Chinese state automatically passed to the Italian authorities, while private owners kept the ownership of their rights, unless the Italian authorities decided, for reasons of public interest, public hygiene or the government's needs, to purchase private property by means of expropriation. Articles 5 and 8 were the most important ones. The former provided that the transfer of rights to real estate owned by Chinese people could only be sold if authorized by Italian representatives and could not be sold to non-Italian foreigners. To offset this, the latter gave the Chinese Emperor's subjects the possibility to purchase land and live in the concession.

These articles, as regards the rules governing property rights, were designed to encourage Italian entrepreneurial activities; therefore, the political value that the Rome government attributed to the concession was high, because it was Italy's first meaningful achievement in the Far East and placed it on the same level as the other powers, enjoying colonial privileges and appropriating an area whose residents were guaranteed the right to run their economic and industrial activities under the protection of Italian national laws and not those of the Chinese Empire.

The Italian concession was in quite a good location, as it extended for about a kilometre along the banks of the Pei Ho river, meaning that quays could be constructed for shipping. The Tientsin concession was the smallest of the foreign settlements and bordered to the east with the Russian one and to the west with the Austrian one. The area of the concession measured 764.50 mou, or 459,000 m^2 (1 mou equals 666.5 m^2), and there was an indigenous village with about 17,000 inhabitants, who lived in hovels and mud huts in disgraceful hygienic and financial conditions. Aside from this, there was also a railway station belonging to the "Imperial North China Railway", where most of the trading in Tientsin was concentrated, and three areas of land put to different use: one had salt caves and the others were a swamp and a cemetery. The concession was in a strategic position, given that it was between the capital city of Peking and the sea. The military presence of the great powers was, in fact, ensured by the military forces of their respective navies and by their warships, which could carry troops. The problem was that Tientsin was a long way from Peking and even though there was a navigable channel, it was difficult to get close to the gulfs to reach Peking because of a shoal that which kept the bigger ships at least ten miles from land. Given the lack of Italians present, the administration of the concession was initially in the hands of a royal commissioner, who was also a naval officer, and who answered to the Italian consul in China. He was served by eight carabinieri (carabineers) and a marshal, who were responsible for ensuring public order, and by four "natives": a translator, a tax collector, a scribe and a policeman; they constituted the administrative and military governance of the concession (Mondaini 1927, 249; Coco 2017a).

As far as the economic prospects and advantages arising from acquiring the concession of Tientsin were concerned, they were not particularly attractive to Italian entrepreneurs and traders. In order to be able to set up business activities, factories and industrial warehouses, the area of the concession needed converting to be used for manufacturing and trading; this would require reclaiming and levelling the land, expropriating the Chinese village, purchasing the salt quays and removing most of the cemetery (Francioni 2004, 151). These problems were also exacerbated by government delays in preparing a development plan similar to that of the other European settlements, which discouraged Italian economic operators and entrepreneurs from arriving en masse. Before the occupation of this land, the Rome government had already considered making recourse to private initiative to raise the capital necessary to start reclamation and development work for the future of the concession. On 6 December 1901, a project had been signed to establish a "Company for the development of the Tientsin concession", with a group of entrepreneurs led by Giovanni Rizzardi. The company had assets of around 40,000 lb sterling, one-third of which had been paid by subscribers and the rest guaranteed by the Credito Italiano bank, which was keen to be involved in business in the Far East, and by the "Italian Company for Colonial Trade" in Milan.

Once the government had obtained the concession, the company promised the government that it would allocate various funds to make the best use of the settlement's territory, which included "the removal of tombs from the cemetery, the reclamation and levelling of the swamp areas, the building of roads in compliance with European standards and the installation of drinking water pipes" (Francioni 2004, 152). As payment, the company asked for ownership of four-fifths of the land, and as a result became responsible for its direct administration.

This project, endorsed by both the consulate general in Shanghai and the Legation in Peking, was blocked by the opinion of the State Council, which held that a special law needed to be passed by the Italian Parliament to authorize the government to conclude the contract. Having noted the unfavourable opinion of a State body, the government resigned itself to the idea of direct administration, which was entrusted to a royal commissioner who worked in tandem with the Shanghai consulate.

The first steps were taken to improve the hygienic and sanitary conditions (filling in ponds and building sewers) and to provide electric lighting for the roads.

In contrast, it took much longer to draw up a building plan for the concession, because it had to take account of the existence of the Chinese quarter; on the one hand, this discouraged possible Italian purchasers, as they could not engage in speculation relying on a future increase on property prices, and on the other hand because expropriating the village would have a negative impact on the inexpensive management of the reclamation and administration of the territory, since the village inhabitants were both a source of cheap labour for public works and the financial resource of the concession in terms of their regularly paid taxes (Francioni 2004, 153). As a result, the economic, building and social development in the early years of Italian occupation was extremely modest. Dr. De Luigi, an Italian who visited the settlement in 1909, almost ten years after territory had been purchased, stated that up until then the "visible" and most important works were the land reclamation and preparations for building a barracks, the barracks themselves and the installation of a Marconi telegraph system to correspond with Italian ships and with the Peking Legation (Mondaini 1927, 249). As regards economic and social measures, there were two thorny issues that immediately troubled the Italian authorities. The first one was the financial settlement requested by the salt merchants and the second was the adoption of the tariff for expropriating private Chinese land; the former was resolved without too much difficulty, but the latter inevitably led to friction with the Chinese authorities.

These difficulties stemmed from the fact that while the concession's lands had passed from China to Italy, Article 5 of the concession treaty established that the Chinese residing there maintained ownership of the real estate. This was further aggravated by the uncertainty surrounding a clear and definitive concept for the development and exploitation of the concession, for which the necessary funds had yet to arrive from Italy. The chance of ensuring economic development in the area was thrown away, because the work needed to modernize the railway and improve the navigability of the river that ran alongside the concession was not done. This uncertainty also stemmed from the fact that no Italian State law had ever approved the 1902 agreement: the decision was justified above all by the fact that it involved no economic or financial burden for the State's central budget, since both the annual rent to be paid to China and the expenditure for managing the concession were to be covered by collecting taxes and by the local wealth. It was only in 1912 that, through a legislative measure, the Rome government authorized the granting of 400,000 lire to the royal administration of Tientsin; this sum was refundable and was to be repaid over a thirty-year period (Francioni 2004, 153).

Thanks to these funds, the land reclamation was completed, the village was modernized and the first buildings envisaged by the town planning and building plan were erected.

The Italian town was built in a bend of the Pei Ho river opposite the old Chinese village. Public buildings appeared, such as the Town Hall, the Consulate, the Parlotto barracks, the Church, the hospital, the police barracks and the telephone exchange, with roads and open spaces such as Corso Vittorio Emanuele III and Piazza Regina Elena; a residential area grew up near these buildings, with western-style houses of typical 1920s Italian architecture and surrounded by gardens. In 1930, there were 17 streets, two squares, public school and health buildings, an Italian and Chinese school, public gardens and two sports fields in the concession. It numbered around 7500 inhabitants, fewer than 400 of whom were Italian. It was only in 1913 that the basic regulation for the concession was decided and drafted by the Italian Royal Minister in China, Count Sforza. Yet the Italian township was only officially established one decade later, in November 1923, pursuant to the approval of the "Municipal Statute for the concession" (Mondaini 1927, 251).

The concession ended and the territory of Tientsin returned definitively to China in 1947, under the Treaty of Paris and with the end of Italian colonialism.

In conclusion, in the absence of an effective entrepreneurial boost in the shape of Italian capital or more decisive government intervention to improve the territory, the concession never became a real foothold for making commercial inroads in China and remained unknown to the general public until 1947, when it was returned to China. However, it was also never a burden for the Italian government, since it was able to maintain economic self-sufficiency through the collection of rents, local taxes and so on: this was how it justified the existence of this far-off eastern possession, before there was the desire to carry out a policy of conquest and to achieve international prestige (Francioni 2004, 155).

Article 1 established that the Italian concession of Tientsin was to be governed by an elected municipal administration under the direction of the royal consul or his deputy and under the high command of His Majesty's Legation in China. The administration was to be elected by the Italians residing in Tientsin and by the subjects of other foreign powers owning property in the concession: the active right to vote was therefore not recognized for local Chinese people. Article 2 established that Italian subjects had the right to buy and rent land in the concession, as did the subjects of other foreign powers, but only after the submission of a written declaration, approved and stamped by the respective consuls, with the formal obligation to comply with and respect all the relative regulations issued by the municipal government. In the event of non-compliance, the authorities had the right to expel anyone who broke the law and to put all their real estate up for auction within six months of their expulsion. In contrast with the right to vote, Chinese subjects had the same rights and obligations as regards the ownership of real estate as those of the foreign powers.[14] The other articles referred to the assignment of personal rights and privileges in relation to real estate, as well as to laws relating to the functioning of the concession, which was entrusted to the consulate or to the legation, in the absence of a municipal government. Thus, the role of royal commissioner was not automatically suppressed since it was still the case that, until the government considered that the conditions necessary for establishing a municipality were in place, the concession would be directly managed by the consul of Tientsin or through the intermediary of a regent (Francioni 2004, 154). So it came about that, while waiting for a sufficiently numerous group of resident Italians to justify the transition to a new institutional regime, the consular administration was extended, and it was ten years before an autonomous elected municipality was established. This was symptomatic of the slow pace of development and the lack of Italian interest in its settlement in China.

The basic regulation contained no recognition of the right to vote for the indigenous people, in relation to the election of the administration: this speaks volumes about how the concession was seen as a colony by Italy as well, in line with the stance of the other foreign powers. As far as the laws on cleanliness and hygiene in the concession were concerned, begging and the building of gaming houses and brothels were strictly forbidden, as well as any immoral behaviour that might breach

[14] Historical Diplomatic Archives of the Ministry of Foreign Affairs, Archive of Commerce 1924–1926, Classi 28–52, Italian Concession in Tientsin, Basic Regulation, pp. 3–6.

the decency laws. Opium could not be smoked anywhere (unlike in the British settlements, where it was permitted, within certain limits) and no shop could be opened without a police authorization; public establishments were not free to choose their opening hours as they all had to be closed by 11 p.m., unless they were given special permission to do otherwise by the authorities. This regulation also included the articles relating to vehicle drivers (especially rickshaws), who had to have a licence and were subject to strict laws if they caused accidents through reckless driving, and also to a fine if they did not keep to the left on the road. In order to avoid chaos and confusion in the streets, the authorities forbade any use of the land for merchandise of any kind without prior authorization and those who had permission were required to keep lanterns lit during the night to prevent accidents. No buildings were allowed, even temporary ones, that might hinder free movement, and anybody who caused damage to public works or services would be severely punished. As far as the part relating to hygiene was concerned, no storerooms for gunpowder, saltpetre, oil or other inflammable materials were allowed that might compromise public safety.

In order to make the concession "decent", it was also forbidden to throw rubbish and dirty water anywhere other than the appointed places, or to hang out washing or anything else from windows or balconies overlooking the main roads.

Articles 20, 21 and 22 of the "Regulations for order and hygiene" included rules for dogs, of which there were many in the concession. They had to wear a collar with the name of their owner on it and a numbered identity medal issued by the chief of police. Every owner was obliged to put a muzzle on their dog and walk it on a lead, and to pay a yearly tax of 3 dollars for each dog. Dogs that were lost and not reclaimed by their owners within 24 h were put down by the authorities responsible, while cases of human diseases of an epidemic nature had to be reported immediately to the public safety officer. Those who died from non-contagious diseases had to be buried no later than 36 h after a medical diagnosis had been made, while those who died from infectious diseases had to be buried after all the sanitary measures had been carried out and any relatives or other persons who had been in contact with the deceased had to undergo disinfection procedures.

As far as business was concerned, all shops had to have a sign in Italian and a sign in Chinese; in addition, a licence was granted to open Chinese theatres, although all performances had to end by 11.30 p.m. The regulation for the payment of all rentals was strictly governed through a series of six articles. Anyone who found themselves vested with the ownership or administration of houses had no more than fifteen days to inform the public safety office about the tenants renting such properties and how they were to be used. The same timeframe applied to each household head, who was required to report all the members of their household. It had to be clearly stated in rental contracts that the tenant was required to respect the relative rules laid down by the concession, and a clause had to be included that established a tenant's failure to comply with their legal obligations as a reason for terminating a contract. As far as the concession's authorities were concerned, landlords were morally responsible for the conduct of their tenants, which meant that they could not claim any compensation from the administration if their tenants, having been expelled for whatever reason, did not pay their rent according to the rental contract. The only option for landlords was to pursue their rights with the foreign or Chinese authorities, according to their tenant's nationality. Those who were in charge of managing boarding schools, hotels and hospices of all kinds, both public and private, were obliged to notify the public offices of the names of anyone who stayed in their establishments. All hotels had to keep a register with the name, surname, home town and destination of their guests, together with the day of their arrival and the date they were due to leave. In relation to the expropriation of private properties in the public interest, according to Article 32, the inhabitants were required to observe the following rules:

(a) clean the house and the part of the road in front of it every morning;
(b) keep a light on over the front door of the house until midnight;
(c) no new buildings or repairs to be undertaken without authorization;
(d) no property to be sold or its ownership to be transferred to others;
(e) report deaths and cases of infectious diseases and not bury the dead inside the boundaries of the concession;
(f) they were not allowed to keep firearms or munitions;
(g) they had to request authorization for weddings, anniversaries, and festivities and their respective parades;
(h) each household had to have an up-to-date census record;
(i) anyone driving at night had to have a headlamp switched on.[15]

The last article of this part of the regulation laid down that all infringements were punishable with fines and, in more serious cases, with expulsion from the concession which was then communicated to the consulates if foreigners were involved and to the Chinese law court in the case of Chinese citizens.

As far as taxation on real estate and other assets was concerned, however, the rules were specific and contained in the part of the regulation entitled: "Tax table". Two half-yearly payments had to be made for real estate, for both owned and rented properties, amounting to 3% of gross income, while a tax of 0.5% on the property's value was collected for every 600 m^2 of land. For trading houses, shops, hotels, theatres and street vendors, the rules were left to the discretion of the authorities, which assessed cases individually according to the importance and the impact of the business on the concession's economy. With reference to river trade, a tax amounting to 10 taels was collected for the mooring rights of steamships, to 5 taels for sailing ships and to 3 dollars for any other kind of barge. For Chinese houseboats, the tariffs were lower from the first to the seventh class and according to the kind of licence, and ranged from a minimum of 0.5 to a maximum of 4.5 dollars, and could be calculated on a daily or monthly basis.

[15]Historical Diplomatic Archives of the Ministry of Foreign Affairs, Archive of Commerce 1924–1926, Classi 28–52, Italian Concession in Tientsin, Regulation for Cleanliness and hygiene, pp. 7–11.

Mooring rights for steamships and sailing ships were only valid for twelve days. Anyone wishing to disembark had to first notify the concession offices and collect the necessary licence which then had to be shown to the police.[16]

As regards vehicles, the payments were organized as follows:

- Trucks or motorcycles, per month .... $ 2
- Cars and horses, per month .... $ 1
- Mule-drawn carts with smooth-rimmed wheels, per month ... $ 1
- Mule-drawn carts, with bolted wheel rims, per month .... $ 1.50
- Rickshaws, per month .... $ 0.50
- Two-wheeled handcarts, per month .... $ 0.75
- One-wheeled handcarts, per month .... $ 0.50

There are still various buildings dating back to Italy's "colonial" period to be found in Tientsin. The Chinese government, which had total public ownership of the area, was going to demolish Chinese buildings of recent construction in order to give prominence to the Italian buildings and town planning.

At this moment in history, Italian and Chinese planners are working together on a design in which some buildings will be demolished in order to make room for internal roads that will recreate the old via Trento and via Fiume; there will be underground car parks and a subway exit in the centre of the area, where a large park will be created. Modern buildings and skyscrapers will be located at the edge of the Italian area to provide new housing for those whose houses are to be demolished. The main commercial activities will be housed in an adjacent area, while there will be cultural activities for entertainment and to promote Italy in the heart of the ex-concession.

The Japanese invasion of China and Italy's alliance first with Germany and then with Japan caused irreparable damage to relations between these previously friendly countries, placing them on opposite sides (Minister for Foreign Affairs and International Cooperation 1991, 416, 464, 525–527, 672, 743).

After the Second World War and during the civil war, faced with the evolving military and political situation, Roma decided to await developments; the proclamation of the People's Republic of China in 1949 put the Italian government in a complicated position, caught between the socialist and communist opposition that favoured recognizing the new state, and America's refusal to accept reality. As a result, Sergio Fenoaltea, who had been sent to Peking as ambassador in 1946 to try and re-establish relations with Chiang Kai-shek, returned to Italy. Westerners did not therefore officially recognize the People's Republic of China, while the Eastern Bloc countries did. Italy was aligned with the American position and only established diplomatic relations with Chang Kai-shek's government, which had sought refuge on the island of Taiwan. In the 1950s, in the absence of political relations, China was of great interest to Italian intellectuals. In 1954, the first cultural delegation led by Francesco Flora visited China, followed in 1955 by the second delegation which included Carlo Cassola, Franco Fortini and Carlo Ternari. There were some private

[16]Historical Diplomatic Archives of the Ministry of Foreign Affairs, Archive of Commerce, 1924–1926, Classi 28–52, Italian Concession in Tientsin, Tax table, pp. 17–18.

Italian initiatives, but only in a few sectors, as they were not adequately supported by a broader economic policy; one example was Fiat, which managed to sidestep the limits imposed by the embargo by granting an Austrian company the licences for making cars for export to China. Interest in China was part of a broader plan for international expansion by ENI, the state company managed at that time by Enrico Mattei, whose entrepreneurial realism was the driving force behind all the schemes that led this great Italian company to develop worldwide, and to approach the People's Republic in 1958, which was seen as an enormous and ever-growing market.

Mattei was not the only one with plans for China; there was also the Socialist Dino Gentili, a Milanese businessman who managed to get round the formal bans in the 1950s to set up first Comet (1952) and then Cogis (1958), in which he merged the import-export activities with China of the leading Italian private and public companies (Conenna and Jacchia 1988).

In 1964, France's recognition of the People's Republic highlighted the problem: the political breakthrough for Italy came at the end of 1968, when the Rumor government took on Pietro Nenni as Minister for Foreign Affairs, who was determined to make recognition of China a part of his government programme, which was then followed by a series of actions on the part of entrepreneurs and the government (Meneguzzi Rostagni 2012, 43–44; Marroni 2006; Massimi 2000).

Chapter 6
Italy in China in the Inter-war Years

Abstract In this chapter, the import and export between Italy and China will be examined, within a particular and complex period such as that between the two world wars. It was characterized in Italy by the rise of Mussolini and the fascist government. The accelerated Italian industrialization process following the Great War had become somewhat unbalanced. This disorderly and artificial expansion would have required, at the end of the conflict, a radical restructuring and a renewal of the plans to allow the resumption of peacetime production and the reintegration of the productive apparatus into a market system. In 1922, the political crisis reached a peak in Italy: the March on Rome of 28 October 1922 carried out by the Blackshirts saw the then king of Italy Vittorio Emanuele III refuse to sign the declaration of a state of siege and decided to entrust Benito Mussolini with the task of forming a new government. The economic and financial objectives of the government programme in fascist times, in short, were: (a) to reduce the deficit of the public budget; (b) to pursue a "productivist" economic policy that would provide more space for private entrepreneurship; (c) to make available a greater share of national savings for private investments (even if, despite Italy being a rural country and the exaltation of the myth of the land and the return to the countryside, its economic policy aimed to favour the interests of the great industrial groups) (Zamagni in Dalla periferia al centro. La seconda rinascita economica dell'Italia 1861–1981. Il Mulino, Bologna, 1990, 349–377; Bof in Grande Guerra e primo Dopoguerra (Chap. V, pp. 89–118), Economia e politica economica in età fascista (Chap. VI pp. 119–156), Dalla guerra d'Africa alla seconda guerra mondiale (Chap. VII, pp. 157–186) in L'Italia economica, 2015, 118–119). In 1927, the labour charter was issued, which was the manifesto of the corporate state: economic life, therefore, came to depend more and more on the state. The crisis of '29 involved, among other changes, the definitive crisis of mixed banks, thereby consolidating the process of banking concentration. Moreover, even before the political circumstances underlying the Ethiopian War and the sanctions imposed by the League of Nations, other factors, such as the defence of the gold standard of the lira to the bitter end, contributed to the affirmation of a markedly restrictive policy, which meant that Italy became increasingly isolated from the international market (Petri in Storia economica d'Italia. Dalla Grande Guerra al miracolo economico (1918–1963). Il Mulino, Bologna, 2002, 113–157; Bof in Grande Guerra e primo Dopoguerra (Chap. V, pp. 89–118), Economia e politica economica in età fascista

D. Strangio, *Italy-China Trade Relations*, Studies in Economic History,
https://doi.org/10.1007/978-3-030-39084-6_6

(Chap. VI pp. 119–156), Dalla guerra d'Africa alla seconda guerra mondiale (Chap. VII, pp. 157–186) in L'Italia economica, 2015, 158–159).

6.1 Mussolini and the New Government

The figure of Benito Mussolini came strongly to the fore in the second decade of the nineteenth century. He was a member of the Italian Socialist Party (PSI) and had gained notoriety and a position of strength in the party during the 13th Congress in 1912 in Reggio Emilia. After a brief period working for a minor newspaper, Mussolini was appointed director of "Avanti", the official publication of the PSI. His break with the party came about with the onset of the First World War. When conflict in Europe appeared to be inevitable, Mussolini initially supported the idea of a neutral Italy and wrote an article entitled "Abbasso la guerra" (down with the war), but then, given how the war was proceeding, absolute neutrality seemed a weak line to take and many intellectuals pushed for Italy to take part in the war.

Mussolini was convinced by these interventionists and wrote an article in 1914 in which he criticized absolute neutrality and pushed for the PSI to play an increasingly active part in public life in Italy and the government by adopting a stance of active and operative neutrality for Italy vis-à-vis the war. The party rejected his proposal, however, so Mussolini resigned from his post as director of "Avanti" and founded a new newspaper, called the "*Popolo d'Italia*". In this way, Mussolini was choosing a decidedly revolutionary path and saw the war as the best way to follow it.

Following a brief appearance in the war as a rifleman, Mussolini took over again as director of his newspaper, which had increasingly become the mouthpiece of fighters, manufacturers and those returning from the trenches. By endorsing interventionism, Mussolini was building himself a new political platform, alternative to socialism, which saw the bourgeois, the daring and the futurists[1] as its social base and source of support (De Felice 2000, 5–8).

In order to extend this support base for his claim to power, in 1920 Mussolini placed himself at the head of the Italian Fasci of Combat. This was more of a movement than a party, which often acted on its own account under the orders of a local *ras,* or regional fascist leader (Montanelli 2003a, 70, 2003b). The followers of the Fasci were former soldiers from the urban middle classes who had provided the largest share of men in the war and were now facing the twin problems of inflation and unemployment. Their enemies were the socialists, but not only them: the Church, the monarchy and the parties constituted a real movement against the establishment of that time. It was precisely the revolutionary nature of this new movement that meant it was not initially approved by the old agrarian landowners (De Felice 2000). Yet this same class, afraid of the claims and the occupation of their lands by the

[1]Futurism was an artistic movement that rejected the ideas of the past, especially artistic and political ones. The futurists combined a love for speed, technology and machinery with dreams of a future with industrial cities celebrating man's technological triumph over nature.

communists, began selling their farmhouses and farms, to avoid being expropriated from them in future. The new owners were sharecroppers, tenant farmers and farmers, who saw the "Fasci" (this was the name of the followers) as their guard and they joined them in large numbers, thus making them of a reactionary and violent nature. It was they who began carrying out punitive expeditions, mobilizing teams for this purpose.

The numbers of teams rose rapidly, especially in the north: they went from 88 to 834, and the members rose from 20,000 to 250,000, thus becoming the springboard for Mussolini to seize power (Montanelli 2003a, 71). In the 1921 elections, both Mussolini's party and the nationalist party took seats in the Chamber of Deputies; this was a decisive step towards taking power. After the March on Rome on 28 October 1922, King Victor Emmanuel III decided to appoint Mussolini Prime Minister, who at that time had about twenty members of parliament. As head of a government composed of liberals, nationalists and populists, Mussolini favoured the restoration of state authority and the suppression of left-wing parties, and increasingly identified the party with the state. Up until 1925, Mussolini's actions were not one hundred per cent totalitarian, and the transformation of Fascism into a regime took place over four years, from his speech on 3 January 1925, the day when Mussolini "formalized" the birth of the regime in parliament, to the plebiscite elections in 1929.

Following his speech on 3 January, the first measures he took, helped by the representativeness of the National Fascist Party and its militias, which were incorporated into the army, were to suppress the freedom of the press and to dissolve all political parties. He named himself the *Duce* and claimed the right to issue decree laws and to change the system; in 1929, he amended the electoral law again and called an election that same year, in which there were only 136,000 votes against. At local level too, he replaced elected mayors with podestàs (a medieval term for the leader of a civic government) appointed by the government, and the regime thus became increasingly authoritarian (Romano 1977, 248).

6.2 The Chinese Market for Italy

One of the first important acts of foreign policy carried out in China by the new Italian government was the ratification of the Washington treaties, just three months after the March on Rome. The Washington Naval Conference, held in the American capital between November 1921 and February 1922, had been convened to define the policy to be adopted by the foreign powers in the Pacific area, especially regarding the naval armaments that would maintain their position there, and also to settle the dispute between China and Japan, after the latter had imposed the famous treaty with the "twenty-one demands" on China in 1915 (Borsa 1994, 239).

Italy was interested above all in recognition of its naval parity with France, which it achieved. Together with the other powers, it was also a signatory of the treaty in which the Open Door principle was re-established and reaffirmed, even if this principle meant very little to Italy, since its interests in China at the beginning of the 1920s were really quite modest. For an entire decade, the policy of Mussolini's government was to wait and see. With its new imperialist fervour, Italy seemed more interested in the geopolitical events taking place in the Middle East and in Africa than those in China. Italy continued to align itself with the other powers in China, especially with Great Britain, not because of any conviction or shared interests, but because Italy itself had no specific objectives or purposes. Like the other powers, the Italian government recognized the various military governments that wanted to take power in Peking and also supplied the warlords with weapons. It is important to know in detail what Italy's contribution to the Chinese Civil War was in terms of arms and munitions, also taking into consideration the years before Mussolini took power as well.

In 1917, Cavalier Maurizio Bensa, acting Commander of the Royal Navy's Detachment in China at that time, sent a proposal to the Navy's General Staff Office to set up a sample display of Italian arms and munitions at the Italian Legation to make it easier to conclude contracts with the Chinese government and provincial authorities. The Royal Government approved the proposal and the Ministry of the Navy took on the responsibility of carrying out this scheme. The first Italian steamships began to arrive in China towards the end of December 1918, loaded with weapons to deliver to the Italian Legation, which meant there was no need for government or customs permits. In the meantime, a Peace Conference was called in Shanghai between representatives from the north and south, and with representatives of the powers of France, Great Britain, the USA and Italy acting as mediators.

Italy found itself in an awkward situation, since on the one hand it had to take part in promoting peace, and on the other hand it had to take into account the contracts for the sale of arms that were materializing at that time.[2] In January 1919, an American proposal began to be discussed, which aimed to have all the powers work together to prohibit and prevent their fellow countrymen from selling and exporting arms and munitions to China. In April, Italy managed to conclude two important contracts: one with the military government of Hunan and the other with the province of Szechuan, with the relative initial payments for supplies on account. These contracts established that it was up to the buyers to get an import authorization from the central government and that Italy could only send the arms when these authorizations had been obtained. Again in April, the American proposal to ban the importing of arms into China was accepted by all the representatives of the foreign powers except by the Italian one. The ban literally established that all foreign governments made a collective commitment to prohibiting their citizens and subjects from exporting war weapons and ammunition or any materials for their manufacture to China, until a government was established whose authority was recognized throughout the country, and also to

[2]Historical Diplomatic Archives of the Ministry of Foreign Affairs, Political Affairs Series Inventory 1919–1930, Pacco 951, Fascicolo 2057 bis, Letter from the Royal Italian Legation to S. E. Count Sforza, Minister of Foreign Affairs, Peking July 29, 1920, pp. 1–3.

opposing any deliveries of arms and munitions for which contracts had already been made but not executed during that period.[3]

Based on the orders received from Rome, the Italian representatives in China informed the Chinese government that they were willing to respect the contract on condition that the contracts already concluded were carried out correctly. The Chinese government refused this request, but steamships such as the "Nippon", the "Persia" and the "Gablonz" arrived in Shanghai anyway, loaded with arms.

The unloading of the goods gave rise to a press campaign that was extremely hostile to this traffic and to Italy, which did not accept the dispositions of the Chinese government; unrest broke out in various southern provinces, and the government in Canton informed the Italian Chamber of Commerce in Shanghai that if the traffic did not cease there would be damaging repercussions for Italy's interests. In the early 1920s, Italy managed to conclude, more or less openly, four important contracts with four Chinese leaders, mainly due to the efforts of Major Carlo Pestalozza, who was not the least bit concerned about the ban imposed by the other powers.

Contracts were concluded with four Chinese governors: those of Manchuria, Shansisa, Tachang and Hunan. The contracts contained above all the sale of rifles, grenades and spare cartridges, as shown in Tables 6.1, 6.2 and 6.3[4] (the values are expressed in gold francs).

The orders amounted to 29,959,100 gold francs; some materials that were part of the second and fourth contracts, including a mortar, a howitzer and two cannons, were loaded onto the steamship "Persia" and captured by bandits, while the arms ordered in the first contract arrived safely at their destination on the steamship "Nippon".

China had 440 million inhabitants at that time and its foreign trade amounted to about 8 billion Italian lire. The increase compared with the previous decade had not been large, owing to the difficulties caused by the war. What really altered greatly were the prices of raw materials and basic products, although the difference was offset by the increase in silver and the inferiority of imported goods. China's foreign trade included a huge range of products, ranging from cotton products, metal beds, various textiles, clocks, cutlery and window panes. As regards raw materials and semi-finished products, China exported raw cotton, wool, peanuts, lard, leather, mats, vegetable oils, hides, straw plaits, tobacco and many other items. As far as modern plants for mineral extraction are concerned, statistics show how this sector had also become important in China. To give an idea of this, 5,113,182 *piculs* (a traditional Asian unit of weight) of iron ore were exported in 1919 (equivalent to 60,433 kg) against 4,679,634 in 1916, 2,432,904 *piculs* of metal against 2,392,122 and 689,823 *piculs* of metallic copper against 564,818.

[3]Historical Diplomatic Archives of the Ministry of Foreign Affairs, Political Affairs Series Inventory 1919–1930, Pacco 951, Fascicolo 2057 bis, Letter of the Royal Italian Legation to S. E. Conte Sforza, Minister of Foreign Affairs, Peking July 29, 1920, p. 4.

[4]Historical Diplomatic Archives of the Ministry of Foreign Affairs, Political Affairs Series Inventory 1919–1930, Pacco 951, Fascicolo 2057 bis, Ministry of War-General Directorates of Artillery, Subject: Arms sales to China, Rome March 1921. The report does not have the figures for the third contract for sales in the Governorate of Tachang.

Table 6.1 Italian contracts in the governorate of Manchuria (in gold francs)

1st contract	Governorate of Manchuria
50,000 rifles mod.91, complete with bayonet dagger	4,000,000
50,000 series buffers in fabrics	500,000
50 million shotgun shells (fs 180 per thousand)	9,000,000
64 Fiat automatic machine guns, complete with tripod, accessories and a series of spare parts	288,000
640 thousand cartridges for said	115,200
32 replacement rods for machine gunners	1,600
24 field guns, grouped into six batteries, each on four pieces, 8 chests, a tow truck and spare materials, with complete harnesses for their towing	2,220,000
12 thousand full shots per grenade and 12 thousand at shrapnels	1,320,000
24 mountain guns of 65, grouped together in batteries, each consisting of 4 wells, 120 bonnets for ammunition, bonnets for veterinarians, for health, forges and spare materials, as well as complete harnesses for their towing	900,000
12 thousand full shots per grenade and 12 thousand at shrapnels	780,000
A piece-of-car vehicle for the countryside, complete (body piece, front end, loads, aiming instruments, protection caps, shields)	61,000
Said as above; from the mountain	12,000
200 Beretta pistols	10,000
200 cartridges per weapon	5200
50 thousand haversacks	225,000
50 thousand water bottles	112,500
Total	Fs. 19,550,000

Source Historical Diplomatic Archives of the Ministry of Foreign Affairs, Political Affairs Series Inventory 1919–1930, Pacco 951, Fascicolo 2057 bis, Ministry of War-General Directorates of Artillery, Subject: Arms sales to China, Rome March 1921. The values referring to the III contract (relating to the sale in the Governorate of Tachang) are missing in the report

In the agricultural sector, cotton was the country's most important product, but it was still cultivated using primitive methods. American experts had, however, provided assurance that a scientific selection of seeds could increase production fivefold without needing to extend the land for cultivation. The system could be used to increase the production of silk and of all the other products ten times over.[5] As regards the oil sector, China had five oilfields, mainly located in remote areas with little in the way of infrastructure. One of the most important centres was in Yen-chang, where the extraction from seven existing wells was still carried out using archaic methods, although there was a refinery which produced oil that was good for

[5] Historical Diplomatic Archives of the Ministry of Foreign Affairs, Political Affairs Series Inventory 1919–1930, Pacco 951, Fascicolo 2057 bis, Letter of G. A. Bena, President of the Italian Chamber of Commerce in China, Shanghai 20 October 1918. pp. 3–8.

Table 6.2 Italian contracts in the governorate of Shansisa (in gold francs)

II° contract	Shansisa Governorate
20 thousand guns at 86 lire	1,720,000
20 thousand series buffers at 10.50 lire	210,000
1000 cavalry muskets at lire 94	94,000
1000 buffets at lire 30	30,000
10 million and 500 thousand cartridges at 205 lire per thousand	2,152,500
32 Fiat machine guns at 5000 lire	160,000
320 thousand cartridges	65,600
9 mountain batteries from 65 to 160 thousand lire	1,440,000
7200 grenades at lire 32	230,400
28,800 shrapnels to lire 37	1,065,600
20 thousand haversacks at lire 5	100,000
20 thousand water bottles at lire 2.75	55,000
Total	Fs. 7,323,000

Source See Table 6.1

Table 6.3 Italian contracts in the governorate of Hunan (in gold francs)

IV° contract	Hunan Governorate
10 thousand rifles at lire 86	860,000
10 thousand buffets at 10.50 lire	105,000
10 million cartridges at 205 lire per thousand	2,050,000
6 Fiat machine guns at lire 5000	30,000
200 thousand cartridges	41,000
Total	Fs. 3,086,000

Source See Table 6.1

lighting. The oil trade operated under what was virtually a monopoly system run by Standard Oil and Asiatic Petroleum Co., which had divided up the areas of work and set prices that cut out any competition, as if they were a cartel. Small quantities were imported by Texas Co. and by some Japanese companies, but they counted for very little compared with the two leading companies. However, oil production declined between 1918 and 1922, especially at its most important plant in Yenchang, and so the powers present in China were not particularly interested in this product.[6] It was

[6]Historical Diplomatic Archives of the Ministry of Foreign Affairs, Archive of Commerce 1924–1926, Classi 1–27, Letter of the Real Consulate of Italy to S. E. Hon. Benito Mussolini, Minister of Foreign Affairs, Tientsin, 23 May 1924.

rather the great variety of products and the population increase that meant that foreign countries, including Italy, saw China as the world's largest market of goods to be exploited. All the industrial nations, concerned about the difficulties in procuring raw materials and finding new free markets for their manufactured products, had done everything they could to become firmly established on the Chinese market. Italy, however, had stood back, despite being the nation most in need of finding new sources of raw materials to fuel its industries and new markets capable of absorbing its industrial output.

The Italian Chamber of Commerce had never stopped calling Italy's attention to the compelling need to take an interest in the Chinese market, yet despite such efforts, Italy had still not been able to create a position for itself as a great country in China. Leaving aside countries like Great Britain and the USA, which had been present in China for many years, small countries like the Netherlands and the Scandinavian countries had managed to make considerable headway in China; even Romania had been able to create trade organizations thanks to help from its banks. Only Italy continued to be "absent".

Had Italy wanted to, however, it could have played a leading role and been one of China's main trading partners. China thought of Italy as being different from the other European countries, in the sense that it had no particular political ambitions in the Chinese Republic, so it could and should have taken advantage of this position of privilege. In addition, China and Italy complemented each other as countries. The former had an exhaustible supply of raw materials and a huge population, which guaranteed, in line with development, a constant increase in purchasing power; Italy, which was on its way to becoming a fully fledged industrialized country, would have a vast market for its products in China and import the raw materials needed to fuel its industrial plants at low prices.[7] Yet in order to achieve all this, three elements were needed to be incisive and make commercial headway in China: banks, shipping lines and trade organization.

6.3 The Italian Bank for China

The idea of an Italian bank in China had been around for some time, and in fact on 11 December 1901, there was a convention in Rome attended by the Società Italiana per il Commercio colle Colonie (Italian Company for Colonial Trade), the Credito Italiano bank and the Società Bancaria Milanese (Milanese Banking Company), and the government approved the opening of a banking branch in Shanghai.

Business at this branch was modest, and it was never really successful as a bank; it eventually became an institution for governmental issuance, tasked with guaranteeing money remittances for Italy's Royal Navy ships, consignment services for troops

[7] Historical Diplomatic Archives of the Ministry of Foreign Affairs, Political Affairs Series Inventory 1919–1930, Pacco 950, *Italian Bank in China*, Letter of G. A. Bena, President of the Italian Chamber of Commerce in China, Shanghai, 20 October 1918, p. 9.

and navy detachments and consignment services for the Royal Legation in Shanghai (Francioni 2004, 163). A real national bank was instead necessary, which could act as an intermediary between entrepreneurs and Italian traders, and financial activities on Chinese territory, and was also able to guarantee lower fees and interest rates than the foreign banks already open in China. Another valid reason for establishing an Italian Bank was the difficulty in transferring money, since in the absence of a national bank, money transfers had to be carried out through foreign banks, which meant there was absolutely no confidentiality for Italian businesses.[8] Furthermore, an Italian Bank would mitigate the "harshness" of the exchange between the Italian lira and foreign currencies. Once the bank was open, this steep exchange rate would decrease, as the lira would then appear on China's financial market and be recognized and used for trading.

There were fifteen large foreign banks in Shanghai and so the field of action for banking was extensive. According to the Italian Chamber of Commerce in China, the bank was supposed to have its headquarters in Shanghai, since this city was the centre for foreign industry and trade in China. As trade gradually increased, the bank would then need to open branches in the other large cities too, such as Canton, Peking, Hong Kong and Hankow.

The Chamber of Commerce estimated that about 40 million Italian lire were needed to open the bank, to be subscribed in equal parts by four large Italian banks: Banca Commerciale Italiana, Credito Italiano, Banca Italiana di Sconto and Banca di Roma. The four banks that competed to establish the national bank had to provide, under advantageous conditions, the services of all their headquarters and branch offices abroad, in order to create a substantial means for the commercial penetration of China, with great benefits for Italy's national economy and, indirectly, for its banks.

The Italian Bank for China was meant to create a powerful commercial entity for Italy with its headquarters in Shanghai and branches in all the main trading centres of the Chinese Republic. While dealing with trade exchanges between Italy and China, this institution was also intended to do business with all the other world markets, serving as a Pacific base. The main tasks for the Italian Bank were to promote trade between the two countries, provide a loan service to China, as Italy had agreed with its allies, accept payment of the indemnity that China owed to Italy, promote the creation of Italo-Chinese bodies in order to pursue industrial and agricultural development in China, especially for improving cotton cultivation, and finance activities such as the exploitation of mines, the building of railways and the refurbishment of waterways.

From an organizational point of view, the bank would need to set up a structure similar to that of the large firms located in China, with special departments for each group of related products.[9] Another valid reason for creating an Italian Bank

[8]Historical Diplomatic Archives of the Ministry of Foreign Affairs, Political Affairs Series Inventory 1919–1930, Pacco 950, *Italian Bank in China*, Letter of the Real Legation in Beijing No. 101/13, Beijing 25 January 1919.

[9]Historical Diplomatic Archives of the Ministry of Foreign Affairs, Political Affairs Series Inventory 1919–1930, Pacco 950, *Italian Bank in China* Letter of G. A. Bena, President of the Italian Chamber of Commerce in China, Shanghai, 20 October 1918, pp. 10–13.

was that it could become a very useful, if not essential complement for opening a direct shipping line between Italy and China. It took 13 days to travel from Milan to Shanghai, but the idea was to halve that time by setting up a direct shipping line with no stops, and this was to be achieved by the Lloyd Triestino company. This represented a golden opportunity for the Italian Bank, since it would be involved in all the ensuing maritime trade and all its profits. The Italo-Chinese Bank, which took the name Italian Bank for China, was founded in 1919. In 1925, thanks to the actions of the bank, the Italian government reached an agreement with the government in Peking, which recognized the consolidated debt instruments that Italy had confiscated against Austrian compensation payments and obtained an agreement from the Chinese government that the instalments of the indemnity for the Boxer Rebellion would be made in US dollars through the Italian Bank for China, which applied a 9% interest rate (Borsa 1994, 249).

Italy and other powers, including France and Belgium, had initially asked for the indemnity to be paid in gold, but the Chinese government had refused to pay in that currency. Italy was keen for these payments to be made in gold as many of its countrymen had lost significant sums of money, in the form of interest-bearing bonds repayable over 20 years, following the bankruptcy of the "Banque industrielle de Chine".[10] Payments in gold would have meant that many people would have got at least some of their money back. However, given China's refusal, and an upcoming Customs Conference in 1925 which might mean new tariffs and charges, it was decided to accept payment in paper money, but it would be in dollars and at a high rate of interest.

6.4 Italian Trade in China: 1920–1930

Before analysing the data on Italy's volume of trade in China in the 1920s, it is important to look at the Chinese customs situation and the reform proposals made.

Up until October 1925, when the work of the Customs Conference began in Peking, citizens belonging to one of the powers that had specific treaties with China paid an ad valorem duty of 5% for goods of theirs coming into the country. At the 1921 Washington Conference, the Chinese government had achieved (and at a special conference that took place in Peking from October 1925 until July 1926) an increase of 2.5% in the duty under certain conditions. All national citizens were subject to this duty, if they were from states that, despite it not being stated explicitly in their treaties, enjoyed the same treatment thanks to the most favoured nation clause. As far as the citizens and goods of those states that did not have treaties with China were concerned, they also had to pay an ad valorem duty of 5%, as this duty was applied

[10]Historical Diplomatic Archives of the Ministry of Foreign Affairs, Trade Archives 1924–1926, Classi 28–52, Memorandum: topics of interest to Italy during negotiations with China, Peking 10 December 1924.

taking account of the nationality of the person asking for the release of goods.[11] At the Washington Conference, the foreign powers had agreed on an increase in Chinese customs tariffs of 2.5% on ordinary goods and of 5% on luxury goods. In Peking, the Chinese delegates proposed greater increases in duties: 5% on ordinary goods, 20% on luxury items and 30% on wines and tobacco, and declared that they were willing to ensure that the earnings from higher duties would go towards consolidating bad Chinese loans, a *sine qua non* for re-establishing China's credit.

Like those of the other states, Italy's delegation supported China's desire for a higher autonomous tariff than that agreed in Washington,[12] which would have provided an income of around 90 million Mexican dollars, enough to tackle the consolidation of foreign loans and other administrative expenses. This was also because, despite the application of these increases, Chinese customs were still much lower than those of other countries.[13]

Great Britain was opposed to this and did not want to concede higher customs tariffs than those agreed in Washington, since an excessive increase would damage its trade, and it was only involved in a small share (11%) of the consolidation of bad foreign loans. Italy's interests were diametrically opposed to those of the British, as Italy only provided a very small share of Chinese imports but, after Japan, it was the foreign power that most wanted to have China's bad loans settled. In the end, after several meetings among the delegations, the foreign powers reached an agreement: they were willing to concede, aside from the surtaxes promised in Washington to be added to the 5% already in force, higher scaled surtaxes, from 2.5% up to 22.5%, with an overall annual increase in customs revenue of about 90 million dollars. The powers also accepted the principle of customs autonomy which would enter into force in January 1929. However, all these concessions had to be the subject of a new treaty between China and the foreign powers to replace the old ones, some of which dated as far back as 1842; they were subject to special conditions in order to safeguard their trade, restore credit to boost China's limited finances and offer guarantees sufficient to prevent the new customs revenues from becoming easy plunder for the militarists ruling illegally in various provinces. One of the most significant of these conditions was the abolition of the *likin*, which had never actually been achieved, and the consolidation of Chinese debts. The Customs Conference closed with a failure, the reason for which was the insistence of the Chinese delegates on obtaining everything unconditionally, compelled by a sense of national dignity and refusing to recognize the impotence of the Chinese government at a time of political and military chaos.

[11] Historical Diplomatic Archives of the Ministry of Foreign Affairs, Political Affairs Series Inventory 1919–1930, Pacco 953, Fascicolo 2087, *Customs Conference*, Letter from Dr. T. Cerruti No. 296-93, Beijing March 28, 1924.

[12] Historical Diplomatic Archives of the Ministry of Foreign Affairs, Political Affairs Series Inventory 1919–1930, Pacco 953, Fascicolo 2087, *Custom Conference*, Telegram incoming No. 3635 of the R. Minister in Beijing to the Minister of Foreign Affairs, Subject: Customs Conference, Beijing 5 November 1925.

[13] Historical Diplomatic Archives of the Ministry of Foreign Affairs, Political Affairs Series Inventory 1919–1930, Pacco 953, Fascicolo 2087, *Custom Conference,* Letter from the Italian Bank in China and the Trieste Shipyard to the Ministry of Foreign Affairs, Rome 4 January 1927.

The conference was being held in the middle of a civil war that had lasted for years, and a succession of governments had led to the Chinese delegates being replaced over and over again, meaning that the foreign representatives found themselves faced with a Chinese delegation that lacked any effective or responsible representation. Even the attempt to apply the tariffs decided in Washington failed, despite the foreign delegations putting together and approving a proposal that fully reflected the spirit of the treaty concluded in the USA.[14]

Political difficulties and the lack of a strong and recognized central government in China were some of the obstacles to a review of the customs tariffs; the central customs service was still in force for the legal 5% ad valorem duty, but other surtaxes were imposed, and other, illegal ones were tried out and planned for the future. Specifically, the new Government of Nanking, which took power in 1927, applied a surtax of 50% (later reduced by 25%) on tonnage rights; an ad valorem tax of 30% on alcoholic drinks and of 50% on tobacco; a surtax of 7.5% on all imported goods; a variable tax of between 15 and 25% on luxury goods; and an excise duty on the output of industrial plants such as cotton mills and silk plants, almost all of which belonged to foreigners, especially from Japan.[15]

The customs situation was therefore one of absolute chaos, which caused many difficulties and inconveniences between traders and the foreign consular and diplomatic authorities. Table 6.4 summarizes the various tariffs, legal and illegal, applied by successive Chinese governments.

On the eve of the 1925 Customs Conference which, as we have seen, achieved nothing concrete, the figures for Italy's imports and exports with China were considerably lower than those for other foreign countries, although this had been the case ever since the first Sino-Italian treaty had been signed in 1866 by Admiral Arminjon. According to the statistics published by the "Maritime Customs of China" for the year 1922, Italy imported goods worth 2,318,579 Haikwan taels to China and exported goods worth 6,050,185. However, a comparison with the data for previous years shows that there had been a significant growth in Italy's trade relations. But contrast, if we look at trade movements between China's ports and the rest of the world, Italy had a very small share, if we consider that Great Britain exported 38,507,874 taels' worth of goods, and Germany, in fifth place and last among Europe's industrialized countries, exported 9,804,806 taels' worth.[16]

The increase in Germany's trade had been considerable, and the increase in trade for the small country of Belgium was even more remarkable, while France's share

[14]Historical Diplomatic Archives of the Ministry of Foreign Affairs, Political Affairs Series Inventory 1919–1930, Pacco 962, Fascicolo 2143, The question of Chinese customs, Camillo Fumagalli, s.d., p. 1.

[15]Historical Diplomatic Archives of the Ministry of Foreign Affairs, Political Affairs Series Inventory 1919–1930, Pacco 962, Fascicolo 2143, *Custom Conference—Chinese surcharge rates*, Letter to S. E Minister of Foreign Affairs, No. 2694/99, Subject: Illegal surtaxes of the government of Nanjing, Shanghai, September 14, 1927.

[16]Historical Diplomatic Archives of the Ministry of Foreign Affairs, Archive of Commerce 1919–1923, Classi 5–7, Letter from the Italian Consulate to the R. Ministry of Foreign Affairs, no. 408-n. Spec 45-pos. 12, Object: Italian trade in China in 1922, Hong Kong 18 June 1923, p. 1.

Table 6.4 Value of duties on imports

Import duty, according to current treaties, 5% ad valorem on all goods
Beijing government Starting from January 1927 / 5% duty—2.5% surcharge Southern nationalist government Starting from 1 July 1926 Duty 5% plus 2.5% on ordinary goods and luxury
Southern nationalist government Starting from 1 July 1927 for tobacco products 5% duty, 5% surcharge, 50% special tax: 60% total
Southern nationalist government Starting from 2 August 1927 for wines, spirits and liqueurs 5% duty, 5% luxury tax, 30% stamp tax: 40% total Presently 30% is avoided through an English consular, 35% is avoided through the Japanese and American consoles

Source Historical Diplomatic Archives of the Ministry of Foreign Affairs, Political Affairs Series Inventory 1919–1930, Pacco 962, Fascicolo 2143, The question of Chinese customs, Camillo Fumagalli, s.d., p. 12

of trade was declining. Italy could have played a bigger role in these markets, had it not been for various reasons that curbed any real expansion in trade. Nevertheless, in the late 1920s, internal inflation and the depreciation of the lira against China's currency, pegged to silver, favoured Italian exports, particularly wool fabrics and artificial fibres, without having too negative an effect on imports and allowing the trade balance with China to come close to being balanced (Bors 1994, 249). For the year 1927, Table 6.5 shows the complete details of Italy's imports to and exports from China.

The list of the Table 6.5, even if they refer to the year 1927 and in particular to trade with China, confirms that since the 1920s Italy became the first country in the world to export artificial silk or rayon, and that, with the support of the regime, the production of other types of artificial fibres in textile spinning increased. The source reports in detail the quantities and measures for each type of asset (which are not reported here but are ordered by category of goods); about 55% is given precisely by the export of these fibres (see Bof 2015, 167–168; see, also, Zamagni 1993, 340–343; Zamagni 2010, 1–6).

6.5 The Reasons Why Trade Did not Take off

There are ten reasons why trade between Italy and China did not develop as it might have done, at least up until 1930, although they are not necessarily listed in order of importance:

Table 6.5 Italy's imports from and exports to China, as reported by the Chinese customs office for the months of June and July 1927[a]

Imports	Exports
Aluminium foil	Black bristles
Army clothing	Boiled silk waste from other ports
Artificial silk thread, wool, cotton, silk and artificial cotton panels, artificial cotton poplin ties	Boiled silk waste, Shanghai
Black diagonal print cotton fabric	Braids of white straw
Black diagonal print cotton fabric	Cinnamon wood
Butter	Cotton yarn, grey, Shanghai
Buttons	Cowhides, not tanned
Calcium carbide	Egg white, dried, frozen. Yolk moist
Chemical wood pulp	Fine porcelain tableware
Cigarettes, cigars	Green tea "Hyson" (Chinese green tea) Ningpo, Kiukiang, other ports
Clocks (to put on the wall or furniture)	Hats, buntal fibre
Coloured diagonal print cotton fabric	Lambskin, tanned
Coloured flannel 30 in. × 31 yards	Rabbit skins, not tanned
Cotton clothing fabrics	Raw silk, not re-rolled and not steam-spun, white, other ports
Cotton fabric for clothes, dyed yarn	Raw silk, not re-rolled and not steam-spun, white, other ports
Cotton flannel, dyed yarn 30-in. × 31 yards	Raw silk, not re-rolled and not steam-spun, white, other ports
Cotton goods, unclassified	Raw silk, not re-rolled and not steam-spun, white, Shanghai
Cotton tapestries	Raw silk, not re-rolled and not steam-spun, wild
Cotton velvet	Raw silk, not re-rolled and not steam-spun, yellow, Hankow
Cups	Raw silk, white re-rolled, other ports
Diagonal print coloured cotton fabric	Raw silk, white steam-spun, Hankow
Diagonal print cotton fabric: 33 in. × 33 yards	Raw silk, yellow Hankow steam spinning
Dyed cotton crepe yarn	Raw silk, yellow steam-spun
Embroidery thread	Rhubarb
Fabric for double printed cotton dresses	Rugs
Fabric for dresses	Shelled peanuts
Fabric for dresses	Silk "pongee" Honan, Shantung,
Fabric for dresses	Silk, cocoons, scraps, silk and cotton mixtures
Glazed cups	Silk, spinning, long waste

(continued)

Table 6.5 (continued)

Imports	Exports
Goods, not classified	Silk, waste, long steam-spun, Shanghai
Hemp thread	Vegetable tallow
Malt	White silk, yellow steam-spun
Mineral water	Whole peanuts
Mixed fabric	Wood oil
Mixed, unclassified	
Olive oil, bergamot oil, loose olive oil, lemon oils	
Outerwear	
Printed double cotton, not classified	
Printed double flannelette	
Printing paper, waxed paper, oiled paper, poster paper, similar paper, writing paper, wrapping paper, coloured paper, coated paper, foolscap paper	
Ribbons of dyed Spanish cotton, 64 in. × 20 yards	
Smooth black velvets backed with cotton and cotton satin	
Soda peroxide	
Spanish cotton ribbon: dyed 64 in. × 20 yards	
Spanish cotton ribbons	
Spanish cotton ribbons: dyed 64 in. × 20 yards	
Sparkling wine, Asti, Marsala, other types, vermouth, beer, liqueur, brandy	
Spun silk	
Steel sheets, steel screws, wires, galvanized steel, stainless steel mesh, steel bars, iron screws	
Sterilized milk, condensed milk	
Unclassified woollen goods	
Velvet	
White cotton canvas under 30 in height	
White flannel 30 in. × 31 yards	
Wool and cotton coats, mats, Melton	

[a]The data were provided by the Italian Statistical Office inspected with the official publications of the Chinese customs offices

Source Historical Diplomatic Archives of the Ministry of Foreign Affairs, Political Affairs Series Inventory 1919-1930, Pacco 962, Fascicolo 2143, *The question of Chinese customs*, Camillo Fumagalli, s.d., pp. 14–20

1. the almost total ignorance of the culture, traditions and customs, together with the reasons contributing to the commercial and industrial development of China along its biggest navigable rivers;
2. the systems used by Italian industrialists and traders to handle business matters. Many Italian firms introduced their products into the Chinese market expecting to be paid in advance and then often sent incomplete shipments, thus losing the trust of their purchasers. It should also be pointed out that Italian goods were often unsuitably wrapped and packaged, meaning that the goods for their customers were of low quality;
3. a lack of agencies in China to publicize projects, designs, samples and the prices of various products;
4. people were sent out who knew absolutely nothing about Asian culture, traditions or customs; their mistaken comments and actions helped to create a negative image of Italy in the eyes of the Chinese;
5. a lack of any kind of advertising or publicity to make Italy's products and designs known throughout China, while other countries conducted excellent advertising campaigns;
6. no help or synergies between Italian traders and banks;
7. there was no understanding of the advantages of setting up consortiums and trusts, as the Americans and the British did, in order to lower the prices and reduce the expense of sending out agents and opening agencies. If Italian firms had played a team game, Italy would have been one of the leading countries in sectors such as motor vehicles, spinning and weaving;
8. the disorganization and incompetence of the consular offices in the Far East, which were barely operational and poorly funded;
9. negligence on the part of commercial institutions and associations in requesting economic data and news useful for Italian entrepreneurs and traders;
10. a tendency to ignore advice and suggestions, especially from government representatives, or from those who had lived there for a long time, either to study or for military reasons and knew the territory very well.[17]

These reasons were at the root of a lack of development and an inability to equal the other powers in their volume of trade with China. Things would improve over the following decade, thanks to activism in the aeronautical and naval sectors and to the political actions of one man, the future Minister of Foreign Affairs and Benito Mussolini's son-in-law: Galeazzo Ciano. In 1927, the men of the Kuomintang took power, forming a new government and establishing their capital in Nanking. The foreign powers took advantage of this and set the conclusion of new trade treaties as a requirement for their recognition of the new government, given that many dated back to the early twentieth century and some as far back as the previous century.

For example, in 1905, Italy opened negotiations with the Chinese delegates, but they could not reach an agreement, and so Italy's economic and political relations

[17]Historical Diplomatic Archives of the Ministry of Foreign Affairs, Political Affairs Series Inventory 1919–1930, Classi 5–7, Letter from the Italian Consulate to the R. Ministry of Foreign Affairs, no. 408-n. Spec 45-pos. 12, Object: Italian trade in China in 1922, Hong Kong 18 June 1923, pp. 3–7.

continued to be governed by the provisions of the 1866 Treaty of Arminjon. The treaty that Italy was preparing to sign, following the opening of negotiations in September 1928, was to be considered as a preliminary agreement that defined and temporarily stabilized relations between Italy and China, pending the conclusion of a definitive treaty between the two countries to replace that of 1866. The Italian delegation, and with it the Italian government, did not wish to immediately draw up a preliminary agreement that might be negatively affected by inadequate preparation; they believed it would be better to wait and consider their choices thoroughly before establishing the basis for a treaty of a general nature. Nevertheless, in the end they opted for the formula of a temporary preliminary treaty. The most important points in the treaty were those relating to customs autonomy and extraterritoriality; the principle of the latter was relinquished by Italy in exchange for a recognition of the right to purchase property in China.[18] The preliminary treaty maintained the status quo for Italian subjects, or rather Italian citizens continued to enjoy all the old privileges conceded to foreigners as long as citizens of any other European country enjoyed them too. An important point was the one that meant that China recognized the right of Italian citizens to live, own property and trade in their country. This was of practical value above all for Italy's religious missions, which were already resident in China, as the treaty permanently legalized their status.

As regards trade relations, they would continue to be regulated by the old provisions until the final version of the treaty was concluded.[19] In particular, the most important articles in the preliminary treaty for the parties concerned established as follows: Article 2 of the treaty laid down that the contracting parties had the right to send each other duly accredited diplomatic agents, who were entitled to all the rights, privileges and immunities recognized by international law, and each country could appoint consuls and vice-consuls at any time, who would also have the same rights, privileges and immunities recognized by international law.

Article 3 established a real freedom of trade and shipping between the citizens of the two countries, who could settle in the other contracting party's country without being subject, owing to their trade and manufacturing, to higher fees, taxes, duties and licences than those collected from other nationals resident in China.

Articles 5 and 6: the former regulated the right to purchase and own moveable goods and real estate of any kind, to dispose of them freely, for sale, as a gift, in exchange, or in a marriage contract, will or succession, under the same conditions as for nationals, with no duties, levies or different taxes; instead, the latter established the possibility of managing one's affairs individually or through an intermediary, but in compliance with and respecting the customs laws in China and subject to its

[18] Historical Diplomatic Archives of the Ministry of Foreign Affairs, Political Affairs Series Inventory 1919–1930, Pacco 965, Fascicoli 2155 and 2155bis, Letter of the Italian Legation, No. 1147/204, Pos. A.18, Subject: Mission to Nanjing for new treaty (report of the negotiation), Beijing 3 December 1928, Year VII Fascist Era.

[19] Historical Diplomatic Archives of the Ministry of Foreign Affairs, Inventory Series Political Affairs 1919–1930, Pacco 965, Fascicoli 2155 and 2155bis, Rome Agency—Daily Information Bulletin No. 291, The Italian-Chinese Treaty and Italian Interests, Rome Thursday 6 December 1928, Year VII Fascist Era.

monopolies. Italian citizens were allowed to access courts at all levels of jurisdiction to exercise their rights and defend themselves.

Article 7 dealt with commercial and non-commercial companies (including public and private insurance institutions) domiciled in Italian and Chinese territory, while Article 9 was very important, as it mutually recognized the right to apply the rules deriving only from the national laws regarding customs and to fix their tariffs freely. It was agreed that as regards the sum, guarantee and collection of import and export duties, for everything relating to industry and trade, each party undertook to allow the other to profit from any benefit or immunity that it might have agreed or could agree with a third power.

Article 14 laid down a prohibition on collecting shipping or port duties in the ports of each country in the event of a ship mooring there due to an accident or to force majeure, provided that the ship did not engage in any trade.

Article 18 was interesting, as the contracting parties agreed to implement the international Paris Convention for the Protection of Industrial Property, concluded on 29 May 1883 (later reviewed in Washington in June 1911) and any other international convention relating to licences to which one of the two parties wanted to adhere.

Lastly, Article 21 established that the treaty was based on the principle of perfect equality and of the mutual treatment as the most favoured nation, and that it would only enter into force, even when ratified, when China had concluded treaties on the same basis as for the powers that signed the Washington agreement, so as to apply the same treatment to trade and to Italian citizens as to other foreign citizens.[20]

The new treaty, signed by the Chinese delegates of the Executive Committee of the Chinese Republic's Nationalist Government and by His Majesty the King of Italy's representative, Daniele Varè, Commander of the Order of the Crown of Italy and Officer of the Order of St Maurice and St Lazarus, was concluded on 27 November 1928.[21] While this was not a definitive treaty, it repealed the 1866 Arminjon Treaty, sanctioned Chinese tariff autonomy and, under certain conditions, repealed extraterritoriality rights.

Italy's non-committal approach in China, as manifested by its exclusively wait-and-see policy, began to change early in 1930. One key episode was the Sino-Japanese Mukden incident of 18 September 1931. China appealed to the Council of the League of Nations [22] invoking Article 11 of the Pact, and given that Italy was a permanent member of the council, it had to take a position. After a series of meetings at the Ministry of Foreign Affairs, a "moderate" line of policy was adopted: on the one

[20]Historical Diplomatic Archives of the Ministry of Foreign Affairs, Inventory of Political Affairs Series 1919–1930, Pacco 965, Fascicoli 2155 and 2155bis, R. Legation Beijing, Annex A to Report No. 864/147, 24 August 1928.

[21]Historical Archives of the Ministry of Foreign Affairs, Political Affairs Series Inventory 1919–1930, Pacco 965, Fascicoli 2155 and 2155bis, Royal Legation Peking, Annex B of Report No. 864/147, 24 August 1928.

[22]The League of Nations was an organization for international cooperation created after the end of the First World War: it was composed of the 32 victorious countries, but it was run by a Council of only nine members, five of which were permanent: the USA, Great Britain, France, Japan and Italy.

hand, Italy had to take part in the collective action of the other foreign powers, but on the other hand it wanted to maintain its autonomy and show impartiality towards China.

In December, the League of Nations presented the Lytton Report, drawn up by the same commission, whose Italian representative was Count Luigi Aldrovandi Marescotti. The Italian delegate to the League of Nations spoke positively about the report on 7 December and invited the commission to play a conciliatory role between the interested parties, urging strong cooperation between the various powers to facilitate a Sino-Japanese understanding and lay the foundations for the rebuilding of China (Borsa 1994, 249–251).

Italy had no interest in supporting Japan's claims, given that there was competition between their economies; it was, however, keen not to antagonize China, given that it could obtain economic concessions from, for example, the indemnity debt arising from the Boxer Rebellion.

This was the policy endorsed by the Italian representative in China, Galeazzo Ciano, who confirmed the Japanese "peril" to the Italian economy, especially with regard to the artificial silk trade.

Ciano's presence in China was a fundamental turning point in relations between Italy and China. In May 1927, Ciano had been appointed secretary for the Legation in Peking, but was then recalled to Rome to take up a post in the Vatican City and there he married Mussolini's daughter, Edda. In 1930, he was appointed Consul General to manage the Legation in Peking. He came to the fore by taking part in the collective action of the foreign powers at a time of political tension between China and Japan in 1932 in Shanghai: his work and his prominent role in the mediation through which the other powers intervened at diplomatic level meant that Mussolini appointed him as Minister Plenipotentiary in China. In this role, Ciano laid the foundations for a greater political and economic penetration of China.

The Italian Legation was well thought of as its members were all relatively young and had not taken part in the activities of their predecessors at the turn of the twentieth century. Ciano's objective was to make China the starting point for a more ambitious Italian policy throughout the Far East. An initial opportunity for reinforcing the link between the two countries was the intention of the Chinese government to purchase Italian aircraft.

Ciano had two objectives: to get China to order several aeroplanes and to convince the Chinese government to hire Italian military experts and advisors. To this end, he managed to get Lloyd Triestino to set up a direct shipping line (a problem at the beginning of the century for Consul General Nerazzini) which shortened the travel times between the two countries, and was also able to procure various orders for weapons, bombs, cartridges and so on through the Italian Manufactures Agency, worth about 14 million lire.

Ciano's project was an ambitious one, and in January 1933, he had a project for setting up an Italian aeronautical mission sent to T. V. Soong, the then Chinese Minister of Finance, which envisaged sending five officers and four non-commissioned officers under the command of a colonel. Kung, director of the Central Bank and responsible for coordinating the purchase of war materials and the military reorganization of the Chinese army, was in favour of the Italian proposal. The mission was sent later than planned, because of disagreements in connection with the indemnities for the Boxer Rebellion which were supposed to finance this mission. Ciano had reached an initial agreement in April 1932, but it did not entirely satisfy the Chinese. In July, the two sides met again and this time they were in full agreement: the indemnity was set at 70 million lire, while the remaining part of the debt was forgiven (Borsa 1994, 253–257).

The aeronautical mission was now free to begin, thus inaugurating a new Sino-Italian economic partnership. Ciano's first orders in 1932 were followed by numerous others until the imposition of sanctions on Italy by the European powers because of its aggression against Ethiopia. In 1933, only one Fiat CR. 32 fighter plane was sold to China, but in 1934 business was excellent, as some 50 fighter and bomber planes were purchased from the Fiat, Breda and Savoia-Marchetti companies. In 1935, China also purchased spare parts, machine guns and bombs for a total of orders worth 48 million lire. The increase in orders between 1933 and 1935 was directly linked to the presence of the aeronautical mission, which comprised Colonel Roberto Lordi, head of the mission, Major Nicolò Galante and 12 other officers and non-commissioned officers.

The work of Colonel Lordi was important as it contributed to the reorganization of the Chinese army, the creation of technical infrastructures, the training of Chinese personnel and the foundation of an aeronautical industry in which Italy participated. One important project was the building of a military airport in Nanchang, but before it was completed, Chiang Kai-shek gave Lordi the task of organizing a bombing course for Chinese pilots who were being called on to put down the Fujiang Rebellion that had broken out in 1933 and was led by a group of pro-Communist politicians. In 1935–36, some courses were organized for officials and for the administrative staff, three repair workshops for equipment and engines were built, each one employing 300 workers, and a total of 800 technicians and specialists were trained (Borsa 1994, 263–266). The aeronautical mission experienced a crisis in the summer of 1935, coinciding with Colonel Lordi being struck down by an illness that left him needing a long period of convalescence. There was growing and open discontent in China because of the delays in aeronautical supplies arriving from Italy; an enquiry was opened, which revealed several administrative irregularities.

Further investigation confirmed that Lordi had been taking bribes for the supply of aeronautical goods, and this discovery, despite corruption being practised at all levels in China, led to Chiang Kai-shek losing his liking for the colonel. Political reasons also contributed to the cooling of their relationship. After 1935, the year in which friendly relations between Italy and China were at their peak, sealed by the two Italian Legations becoming embassies, there was a distinct decline. The mission of Professor De' Stefani,[23] former Minister of Finance under Mussolini, served to

[23]In 1922, he was chosen as Minister of Finance by Mussolini; after few months, he headed the unified Finance and Treasury Ministry, because the Minister of Treasury Vincenzo Tangorra had suddenly died. His appointment as a Minister was actually greeted by his colleagues and all the

maintain and recreate that feeling that was so important for the Italian economy and society. "De' Stefani's mission should have lasted one year, from early 1937 to the end of that year: however, given the critical situation in China marked by the civil war and the Japanese aggression, his mission began in March 1937 and ended prematurely in the summer of that same year, soon after the outbreak of the Sino-Japanese War. During the first part of his mission in China, De' Stefani visited various Chinese provinces and met several governors, mayors and representatives in industrial and commercial circles. On these occasions, he delivered a series of speeches that focused in particular on the importance of national reconstruction and unification. While in Nanjing, he spent most of his time studying the situation and discussing his ideas on the commencement of a series of projects regarding the reform of the economic and financial systems with members of the government, army and economic circles. In July 1937, he was invited to attend a series of summit meetings in Lushan at the request of Chiang Kai-shek himself, as a result of the serious political situation that arose after the Chinese leader's kidnapping by some Nationalist generals in Xi'an at the end of 1936" (De Giorgi and Samarani 2018, p. 167). "After returning to Italy, De' Stefani strove to keep alive the feeble hopes of the ability of Italy and China to maintain a friendly relationship, carrying on a mediation attempt in close cooperation with Jiang Baili during the autumn of 1937. On that occasion, De' Stefani and Jiang Baili agreed upon a draft proposal to be submitted to the attention of Ciano that envisaged Chinese recognition of Italian sovereignty over Ethiopia and the Italian commitment to sustaining the principle of the self-determination of the Chinese people. Thus, it was intended in particular to reassure Chiang Kai-shek that the recognition of the Italian invasion of Ethiopia had nothing to do with the recognition of the Japanese invasion of China. Nevertheless, it is known that this project soon failed due to Japanese intransigence as well as to the uncertainty and ambiguity of the European positions, especially that of Great Britain, which should have played the important role of mediator (See footnote 10). Nevertheless, in spite of this failure, De' Stefani maintained a sympathetic attitude towards China, though not so explicitly, and especially towards Chiang Kai-shek, something that was at odds with Italy's pro-Japanese policy" (De Giorgi and Samarani 2018, p. 167).

---

members of the Association Antichi Studenti with much pride. In Spring 1925, De' Stefani was forced to resign from his appointment due to conflicts with Italian entrepreneurial circles and with Mussolini himself, which sharpened after the murder of socialist leader Giacomo Matteotti in June 1924 by a fascist hand. He was soon invited to teach at the newly inaugurated Faculty of Political Science of the University of Rome. During the following years, De' Stefani's primary commitments were teaching and research. Even though he was invited to join the Grand Council of Fascism in 1932, this did not mitigate his contrasts with numerous sectors of the regime, which were critical of his sympathy towards England and his reservations about racial policy (De Giorgi and Samarani 2018, pp. 164–166). It is within this context that the possibility of De' Stefani's appointment as adviser to the Government of China, whose main purpose was to contribute towards the reform and restructure of the administrative, economic and financial apparatus, became a reality in the latter part of 1936. De' Stefani's name was likely proposed to Nanjing by Hjalmar Schacht (De Giorgi and Samarani, 2018, 166; Historical Archive Bank of Italy, Carte De' Stefani, 30, fasc. 1 *Lettera di Alberto De' Stefani al Generalissimo dopo avere lasciato la Cina*).

Italy's attack on Ethiopia, the intervention of the League of Nations and the application of sanctions caused relations to worsen considerably.[24] The Chinese wanted Italy's actions to be condemned and punished, because this would help to establish a favourable precedent for China with regard to Japan, and this is why China voted strongly in favour of sanctions. In 1937, the onset of the Sino-Japanese conflict marked a further deterioration in relations. As De' Stefani wrote in a letter addressed to the "generalissimo" after Italy's exit from the League of Nations, decided by the Grand Council of Fascism on 11 December 1937 following the economic sanctions against Italy, and decided by the League itself on 18 November 1935 due to the Italian conquest of Ethiopia, the European political balance had changed, due to the new foreign policy directives of some states that were part of the League of Nations.[25] To these, it was necessary to add "the growing development of regimes of authority in opposition to parliamentary regimes and the spread of the struggle against communism and capitalism and the accentuation of anti-Semitic politics".[26] These circumstances, in addition to the rapid spread of the principles of Fascist and Nazi internal politics, led to the weakening of the League of Nations itself, as a guarantor of European and world political balance. De' Stefani, therefore, hoped for a moral commitment on the part of those countries outside the Sino-Japanese conflict in order to avert foreign interference and strengthen commercial ties (referring to the Sino-Italian ones, the strengthening of which was also requested by the national press.[27]

China hoped to hinder the rapprochement between Italy and Japan that had taken place over the previous two years by trying to re-establish economic partnerships, offering the position of Head of China's Air Force to an Italian, Silvio Scaroni, and asking for 50 Fiat fighter planes and 20,000 bombs to be supplied by Italy's Air Force Ministry. However, the Italian government had already chosen in favour of Japan; it refused the request for military supplies and warned Scaroni not to accept China's offer (Borsa 1994, 274–277).

In the early 1930s though, Galeazzo Ciano had worked on trying to set up various joint projects: as we have seen, the aeronautical mission went well, at least initially, as it contributed to supplying various war materials to China. Other projects, despite the goodwill accompanying them, were not so fortunate.

---

[24]The invasion of Ethiopia shattered the Italo-French-British agreement, upon which peace in Europe had been founded up until then and caused the League of Nations to impose economic sanctions on Italy in 18 November 1935 in response to its violation of international law; there was a ban on supplying Italy with weapons and munitions, on granting loans to Mussolini's government and on importing goods from and exporting goods to Italy, especially for use by the war industry. Starting from the embargo period, commercial trade altered in favour of Hitler's Germany, with which Italy was increasingly linked at political level through the 1936 Rome-Berlin Axis and the 1939 Pact of Steel.

[25]Historical Archive Bank of Italy, Carte De' Stefani, 30, fasc. 1 Letter from Alberto De' Stefani to *Generalissimo* after leaving China.

[26]See Footnote 25.

[27]Historical Archive Bank of Italy, Carte De' Stefani, 28, fasc. 6, newspaper clippings, "Il Sole. Giornale del Commercio, dell'Industria, del Finanza e dell'Agricoltura", Thursday 4 February 1937, a. XV.

On 13 July 1931, there was an important meeting in Rome between Soong, the Chinese Minister for Foreign Affairs, and Mussolini. Soong had already visited the other European capitals in order to obtain funding and materials for the reconstruction work in China. Soong presented a project for Sino-Italian cooperation to Mussolini, the key components of which were: Italy would supply warships and merchant ships; it would also supply equipment for land reclamation; and it would transfer industrial plants to China. This all had to be financed by a loan of 500 million lire from the Italian government and Italian industries. The Minister of Finance immediately raised objections to funding the building of hydroelectric plants and land reclamation, as well as to transferring entire industrial plants to China, owing to Italy's chronic lack of capital. Furthermore, the plan for economic cooperation was never implemented because of Japan's veto; the main reason why the Chinese tried to obtain foreign capital was actually to make alliances against Japan.

In 1934, therefore, three years after the meeting and given the impossibility of cooperation at government level, China invited Italy to work together using private companies for the restructuring of the Chinese silk and artificial silk industries.

Some collaborative schemes were presented for building depots and quays, together with hydraulic and electrical projects. The best prospects seemed to be in the silk and hydroelectric plant sectors. Despite having the support of the Italian delegation in China, these projects remained on the drawing board, apart from a few small works. The Italians lacked not only capital, but also the entrepreneurial spirit needed to face competition. In addition, Italy's Minister for Foreign Affairs, while recognizing the excellence of the project, made it known that Italian participation was out of the question at that time because of the perplexities of the interested parties and the inadvisability of exporting capital (Borsa 1994, 261).

As far as the hydroelectric plants were concerned, nothing was achieved because of the disagreements between the Italian technician and the technical bodies of the League of Nations over the exploitation of the waters of the Yangtze River; as regards naval supplies, very little was done as, after managing to sell two motorboats and submarines through Fiat to the secessionist government in Canton in 1934, Italy did not want to commit itself to long-term financial plans to supply steamships as requested by the new government in Nanking. The projects for silk did no better, owing to disagreements relating above all to the co-partnerships of Italian and Chinese firms for setting up a mixed Italo-Chinese company to manufacture rayon (cellulose nitrate). On examining the number of workers in the various production sectors, the census of 1937 showed some differences compared with a decade earlier: there were 4,273,000 workers in total, over 80,000 more than in 1927. The mechanical sector was in first place with 25% of the total number of industrial workers, overtaking the textile sector, which had shrunk during the crisis of the 1930s (from 23 to 17.6% of workers); the food sector was next, having increased from 11.4 to 14%. There were also more workers in the chemical sector, while the metallurgical sector recorded a significant decrease in its workers. The growing use of mixed fabrics, containing high levels of artificial fibres, was also important, the manufacture of which grew significantly during the years of autarchy.[28] Snia SpA, belonging to Riccardo Gualino, a Piedmontese financier and a friend of Giovanni Agnelli, stood out in this area of production. It had made Italy the world's leading exporter of artificial silk or rayon, a fibre made from cellulose. Having survived the crisis of the 1930s, Snia SpA, which was regarded as an autarchic industry par excellence, devoted itself to manufacturing Italian cellulose and was the first to produce this staple, a fibre that could also be used by traditional textile industries. It was supported by the Fascist government which in 1938 obliged the textile industry to use a percentage of rayon and other artificial fibres in the spinning of textiles.[29]

[28]Even before the political situation underlying the war in Ethiopia and the sanctions imposed by the League of Nations, other reasons such as the determined defence of gold parity with the lira played a part in the emergence of a markedly restricted stance, which caused Italy to be increasingly isolated from the international market. Its autarchic policy was in any case consolidated in connection with the economic sanctions imposed by the League of Nations after the attack on Ethiopia. The idea was to guarantee economic self-sufficiency, the start of which can be traced back to the speech made by Mussolini on 23 March 1936 to the National Council of Corporations. On that occasion, Mussolini underlined that autarchy should not be considered as a transitory need because of the sanctions, but should become a distinctive feature of the national economy.

[29]In 1939, it became Snia Viscosa and had a virtual monopoly on the manufacturing of rayon (Cerretano 2004, 2018).

Chapter 7
Evolution of Commercial Relationships

Abstract This chapter gives an overview of what the end of the Second World War entailed, the difficulties and changes faced by the two countries within the new world order that was emerging after the war, and how these influenced a more convinced recovery relations between the two countries to the present day. Before the communist party came to power, the Chinese economy had only undergone sporadic modernization. The Soviet Union provides the new regime, which increased the sphere of socialist influence to about half a billion people, both as a development model and as a source of financial support. But as early as the end of the 1950s, doubts about the relevance of the model lead, on both sides, due to political and ideological frictions, to the 1960 breakup originating on the Chinese side. The communist leaders, once the destruction linked to war (first against Japan, then the civil war between nationalists and communists) had been repaired, found themselves having to face questions concerning development, ranging, from how to finance investment to which industrialization strategy to adopt and to which role to give to the peasant class. Italy also had to face up to a tough post-war period and will resume its economic and commercial relations with China after 1969, with official recognition as a People's Republic.

7.1 Development of Italy–China Trade Relations in the 1970s and 1980s

After the tragic world conflict, in Italy, among other problems, a debate began on trade policy, or rather on the broader problem of Italy's reintegration into the international economy, after the long "isolationist" experience of the autarchic period (Cavalcanti 1984). Such choices would depend on the new international economic balance.

As for the specific relations with China, the People's Republic was officially recognized by Italy in 1969 with a declaration by the Minister for Foreign Affairs, and the following year the two countries signed a joint statement to re-establish the diplomatic and economic relations interrupted during the war years, although there had already been some positive signs prior to this step. In 1964, an agreement had been signed between the Chinese Deputy Minister for Trade and the representative

D. Strangio, *Italy-China Trade Relations*, Studies in Economic History,
https://doi.org/10.1007/978-3-030-39084-6_7

of the Italian Institute for Foreign Trade which approved the opening of a trade representation office in the two capital cities: this would play an important part in increasing and promoting trade and cultural exchanges between the two countries.

Once the economy had restarted, China moved progressively towards the path traced by influential soviet economic thinking that provided both ideological and theoretical references, as well as organizational principles. The collectivization of agriculture proceeded slowly to begin with, but in July 1955, Mao Zedong accelerated the formation of cooperatives and, by the end of 1956, practically the whole peasant class had somehow become part of them. In 1952, the State Planning Commission was created, together with the State Statistics Office, which drew up a national accounting system directly borrowed from that of the Union of Soviet Socialist Republics (USSR), and some specialized economic ministries. The first five-year plan (1953–1957) corresponded to a very rapid period of growth in which priority was given to the development of heavy industry, inspired by the desire to make China a complete and autonomous economic power. This required a considerable commitment to investment, financed by direct withdrawals and indirectly by agricultural products, whose prices were kept very low (the priority given to the development of heavy industry neglected the constraints imposed by the shortage of capital and the overabundance of labour) (the priority given to the development of heavy industry neglected the constraints imposed by the shortage of capital and the overabundance of labour). The end of the first five-year plan inaugurated a long period of instability for the Chinese economy (Lemoine 2005, 15). Pushed by Mao Zedong, ideological concerns began to break into the economic debate. The first five-year plan had reached a dead end as agricultural conditions constrained industrial growth. In 1958, the Great Leap Forward and the creation of popular communes reflected the will to overcome social, technical, economic and financial constraints in order to be able to start transforming the country. The human cost of the crisis that followed this process was staggering: the years between 1959 and 1962 witnessed a ruinous famine that would result in the death of millions of people. This number increases if we also add the effects of the decline in birth rates caused by malnutrition. Industrial production also collapsed in 1961. This period, 1959–1961, subsequently gave rise to a more prudent and moderate economic policy. The authorities focused on material incentives, scientific and technical education, and qualitative and not merely quantitative criteria in evaluating production. From 1965, the *cultural revolution* began in earnest, which would determine a series of changes that called for the radical transformation of Chinese society by means of the fervour and revolutionary ideals present in the thought of Mao Zedong. The *cultural revolution* did not provoke an economic crisis comparable to that which had followed the failure of the great leap forward; it did, however, hold back the momentum that the Chinese economy had gained towards the mid-1960s. The biggest repercussions stemmed above all from the waste of human capital. Almost an entire generation found itself without higher education. The universities closed in 1966 and would only gradually resume their activities from 1970 onwards, with limited programmes, on which politics had a considerable influence. Between 1970 and 1978, politics became less and less violent, but before and after the issue of Mao's succession was decided (he died on 9 September 1976), waves of instability were generated. In 1975, Deng Xiaoping, vice-president of the Central Committee of the Party, presented an industrial plan aimed at encouraging the rigorous management of companies and the systematic use of imported technologies, with the aim of improving living standards. In 1978, the new Prime Minister Hua Guofeng, with the plan for 1978–1985, announced a new economic era for China that foresaw considerable developments in industry. However, this programme would be short-lived (Lemoine 2005, pp. 18–19; De Antonellis 1977). In December 1978, the Central Committee plenum replaced it with a policy of readjustment from its more modest objectives and with a first draft of economic reform. The 1978 reforms did not derive from an overall vision but merely aimed to relaunch production and productivity. Their effects, however, propagated and set in motion cumulative changes and, in little more than twenty years, their dynamics had irreversibly transformed the economic system.

In the 1980s, the change in the global economic system after the end of the Golden Age and the economic crises of the 1970s, which had laid the foundations of what is known nowadays as globalization, the change in leadership in China and the new policy of openness and modernization all led to an increase in imports from abroad, especially of machinery and technology, in order to accelerate the development of domestic industries and make them competitive.[1] There was also an increase in imports of industrial technological equipment from Italy in the years 1983–1987 (Fig. 7.2) compared with the 1970s (Fig. 7.1). Starting in the 1990s, trade with Italy increased significantly in absolute terms, but in 2004 it only accounted for a share equal to 1% of total Chinese trade. Italy was still importing more from China than it was exporting to that country, resulting in a net trade deficit. As can be seen in Fig. 7.3, imports grew from year to year at an average rate of 30%, while exports soared from 1992 to 1993 but then levelled out between 1994 and 1999, with a moderate growth of around 5% (Fig. 7.4).[2]

On the basis of Eurostat data referring to 2018, Italy was confirmed as China's fourth supplier among European countries, with exports amounting to €13.2 billion (−2.4%). This figure, despite the positive results found in the other main sectors, was affected by the decrease of €1 billion (€768 million; −57.6%) in the automotive sector. Italy (€30.7 billion; +8.1%) ranks fourth among China's European customers. The increase in imports has had a decisive impact on the increase in both trade and the trade deficit. The establishment of the Italy/China Business Forum (inaugurated by the two heads of government in June 2014 and relaunched at the beginning of 2016) represents an innovative interaction platform with enormous potential (see Figs. 7.7 and 7.8). The growth of Italian imports (+€2.3 billion) mainly concerns the materials and electrical equipment sector (+€1.2 billion) and, more specifically, the imports of telephone equipment (Embassy of Italy–China 2019).[3] By considering statistical data for China and converting the values from USD to the Euro at an average exchange rate of 1.1367, for China there is an increase both in imports

[1]Van der Wee (1989), Eichengreen (2007), Findlay and O'Rourke (2007).

[2]Further details in Appendix Table A.1 (Fardella and Prodi 2017).

[3]http://www.infomercatiesteri.it/public/schedesintesi/s_122_cina.pdf.

Fig. 7.1 Italy–China imports and exports, 1970–1979 (in millions of euro). *Source* ISTAT database www.coeweb.istat.it

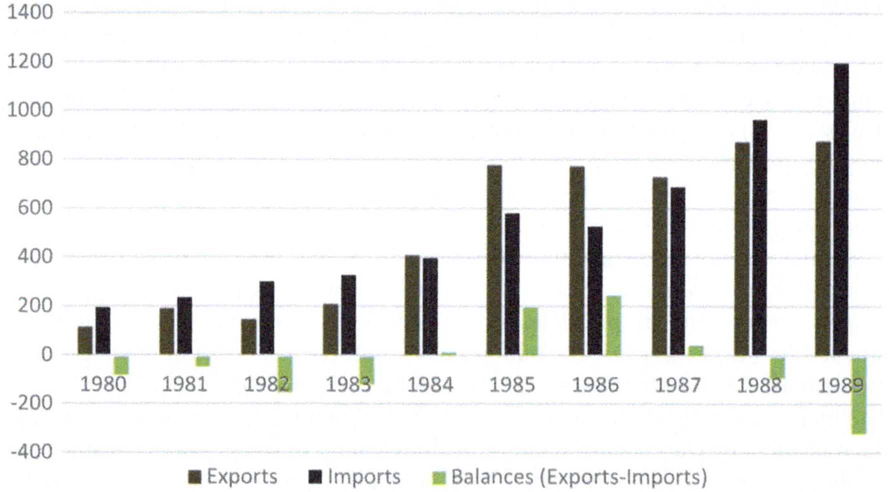

Fig. 7.2 Italy–China imports and exports, 1980–1989 (in millions of euro). *Source* ISTAT database www.coeweb.istat.it

(€18.5 billion; +3.1%) and in exports (€29.2 billion; +13.7%), which is reflected both in the interchange (€47.7 billion; +9.3%) and in the positive balance for China (€10.6 billion; +38.5%).[4] China has been experiencing significant growth for years,

[4]See also Teso 1923; Chen 2000; Brivio 2006; Secchi 1977. http://www.infomercatiesteri.it/public/rapporti/r_122_cina.pdf.

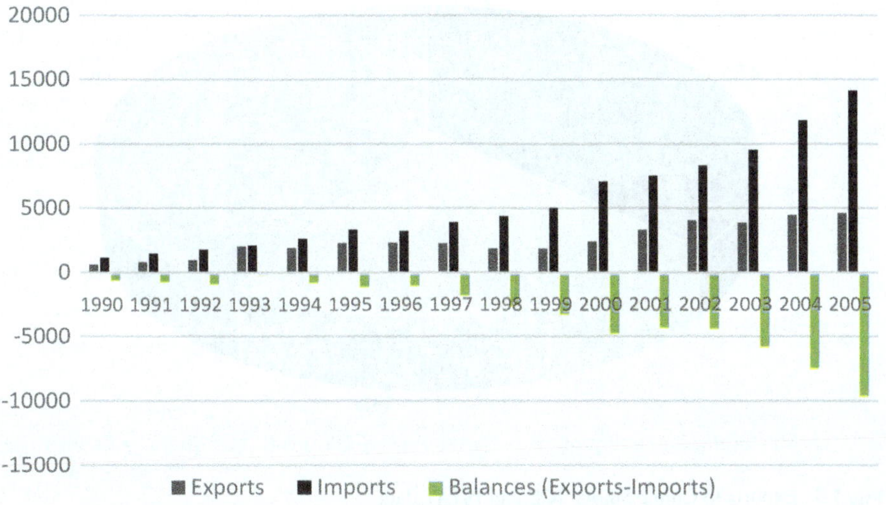

Fig. 7.3 Italy–China imports and exports 1990–2005 (in millions of euro). *Source* ISTAT database www.coeweb.istat.it

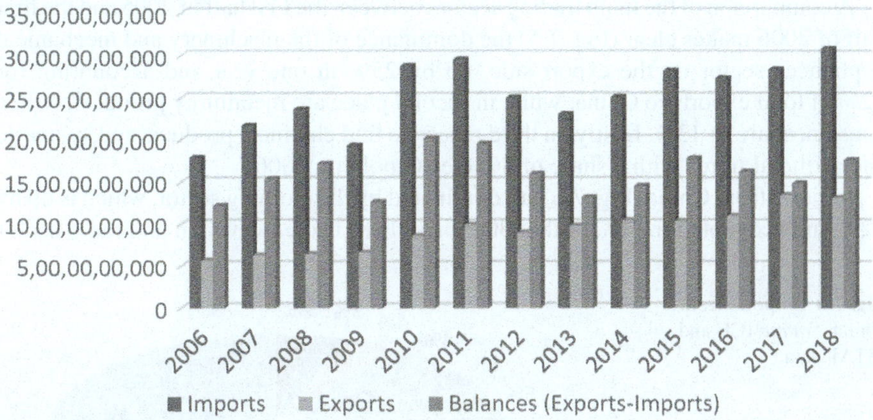

Fig. 7.4 Data of the Export-Import of Italy towards China (2006–2018) (millions of euros). *Source* ISTAT database www.coeweb.istat.it

although its growth of 6.6% in 2018, slowing from 6.8% in 2017 marked the lowest annual growth rate in recent years.[5]

In the first two months of 2019, according to what reported by the National Bureau of Statistic (NBS), the Chinese economy has generally remained stable as far as the main ones are concerned economic indicators. According to IMF estimates, the GDP

[5]http://www.infomercatiesteri.it/scambi_commerciali.php?id_paesi=122.

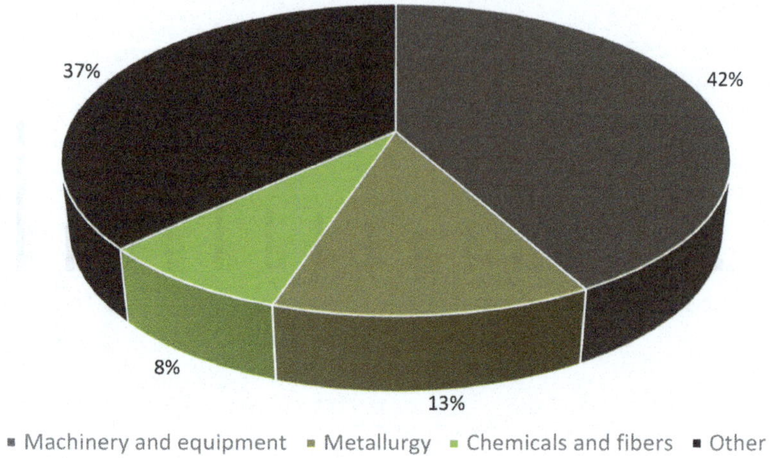

Fig. 7.5 Exports to China. *Source* ICE and ISTAT data

growth rate should be at the end of the year at 6.2%, a level significant given the general context.[6]

A comparison of the main trading sectors between the first half of 2005 and the first half of 2006 makes clear (Fig. 7.5) the dominance of the machinery and mechanical appliances sector on the export side, up by 25% in one year and accounting for 42% of total exports to China, while in second place are metallurgy products, with a constant share of 13%. Lastly, in third place we find chemical products and synthetic and artificial fibres with a share of 8% (see Cipolletta 2006).

Imports from China (Fig. 7.6) are dominated by the clothing sector, which is up by 22% and accounts for 11% of the total; then there is the television and radio sector

Fig. 7.6 Imports from China. *Source* ICE and ISTAT data

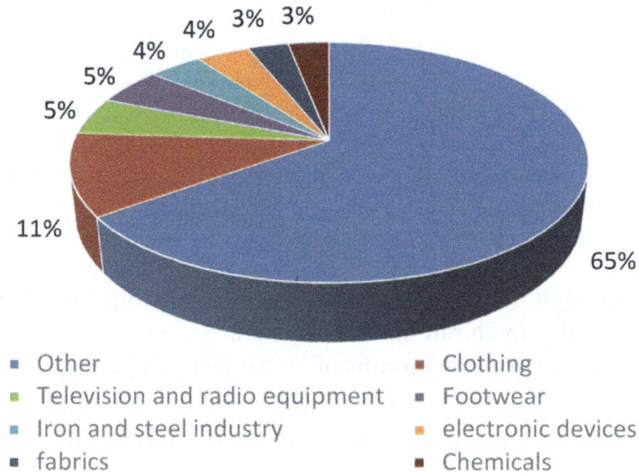

[6]http://www.infomercatiesteri.it/public/rapporti/r_122_cina.pdf.

with an increase of 33% per year and a share of 4.7%, followed by the footwear sector which has recorded the biggest yearly increase of over 43%, and with a share of 4.6%.[7]

The governments of Italy and China now have an agenda focused on strong priorities of the two economic systems. Green technologies, agrifood, sustainable urbanization, health services and aerospace are fields in which Italy and China can invest with the awareness of a perfect complementarity between the Italian technological and industrial capacities in these sectors and the needs of the extraordinary Chinese development (see Figs. 7.7 and 7.8). The impressive urbanization and the growth of the purchasing power of the middle class are the basis for the constant growth of domestic consumption. This is not only in the so-called first cities band (Beijing, Shanghai and Canton) but also in those of second and third bracket (20 metropolises, each with 7–10 million inhabitants), as well as numerous other urban areas of 3–5 million inhabitants. The establishment of the Italy/China Business Forum (inaugurated by the two heads of government in June 2014 and relaunched at the beginning of 2016) represents an innovative interaction platform with enormous potential. The Business Communities of Italy and China have a provision of a permanent forum previously non-existent which joins the intergovernmental dialogue, to facilitate exchange of information, knowledge, industrial proposals and reciprocal investments, including strategic partnerships also on third markets. The last plenary meeting of the Italy/China Business Forum took place in Rome on 22 March 2019 on the occasion of the president's visit Chinese Xi Jinping.

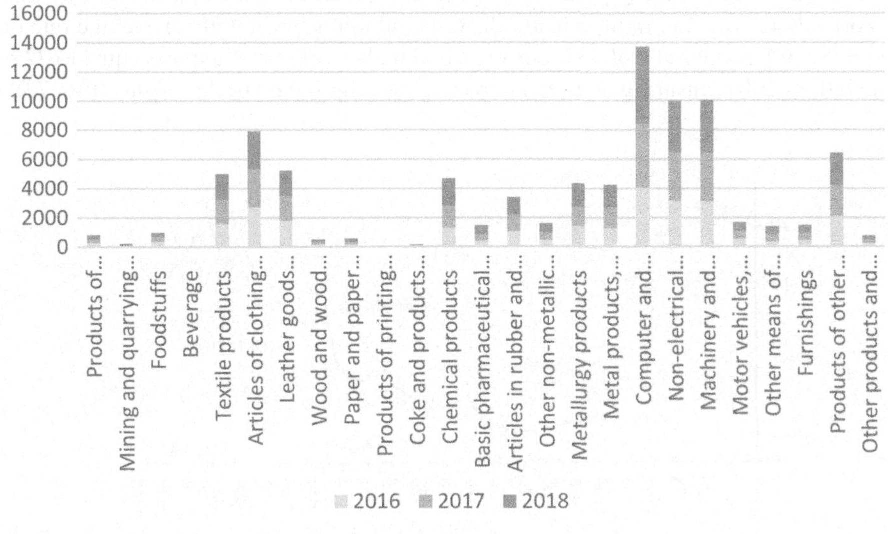

Fig. 7.7 Imports from China. *Source* ICE and ISTAT data

---

[7]Further details in Appendix, Table A.1.

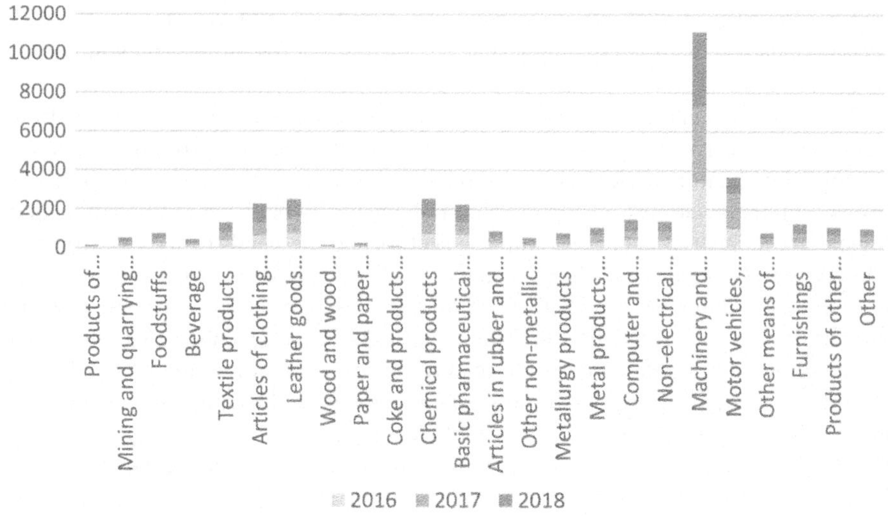

Fig. 7.8 Exports from China. *Source* ICE and ISTAT data

7.2 China's Economic Relations with Italy and the Rest of the World

The 1990s were a turning point for the Chinese economy[8]: the approved economic reforms bore fruit and light industry drove economic growth with an average rate of increase in foreign trade of 15% per year, and with a volume of exports equal to 22% of GDP in 2001, ensuring an ever-increasing and significant trade surplus (Fig. 7.9).

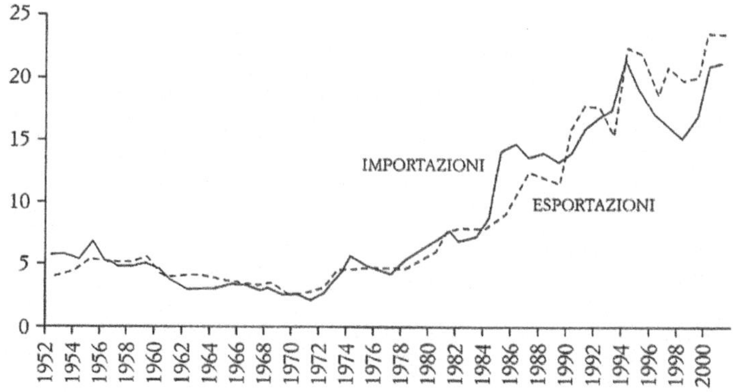

Fig. 7.9 Share of foreign trade as a percentage of GDP. *Source* China Statistical Yearbook

[8]Lemoine (2005, pp. 95–120 and 121–134), Rinella (2006), Chiarlone and Amighini (2007).

There were profound changes in the product-mix of exports in these years in response to the new needs of the global market: the most prominent sectors used to be textiles and clothing, but they have been replaced by the electrical and electronics sectors, whose products recorded one of the fastest growth rates in the 2000s (see data in Appendix Table A.1; Sessa 2006, 2010; Spalletta 2006; Picchio 2006a, b; Pedretti 1977).

7.2.1 The Agreement with Jiangsu Province

Italy needed to catch up with other European countries, such as France and Germany, which had long been committed to penetrating the Chinese market, and it had to try and increase its presence there by taking its firms beyond its national borders.[9]

Italy's industrial system tried to adapt itself to meet growing demand by launching a reorganization of its production and orienting it towards new standards in order to conquer China with high-quality products and with more value added in terms of innovation, research and better services.

The flourishing province of Jiangsu (see Maps 7.1 and 7.2), located along the central coastline and with Nanjing as its capital, is one of the most dynamic areas as regards economic growth in China; it alone accounts for 11.7% of GDP and has the

Map 7.1 Province of Jiangsu, reprocessing by Augusto Frascatani, Department Memotef Sapienza University of Rome

[9]ICE (2006).

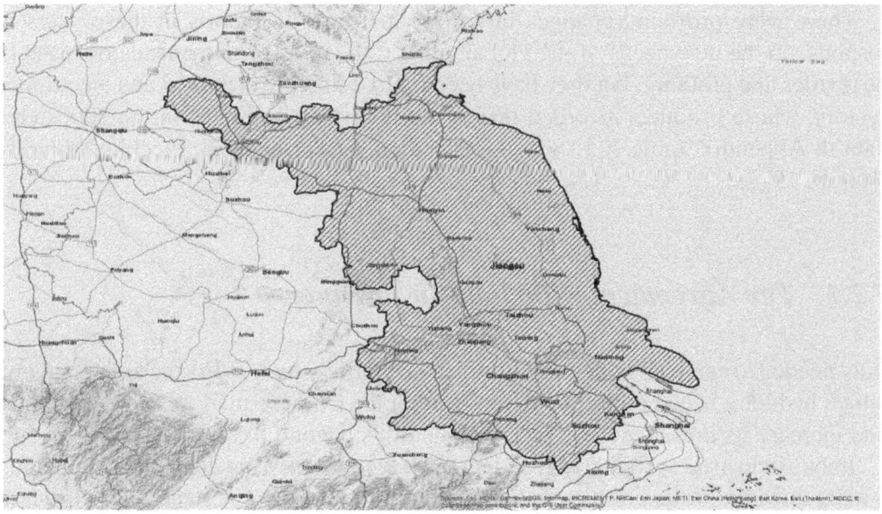

Map 7.2 Province of Jiangsu, reprocessing by Augusto Frascatani, Department Memotef Sapienza University of Rome

highest inflow of foreign investment and the second highest volume of commercial trade with an increase in 2005 of 33%.[10]

The government of Jiangsu has set up a preferential channel for Italian firms interested in investing there and provides administrative and bureaucratic assistance and support. Over the years it has drawn up a calendar for an exchange of visits for representatives of Confindustria and the government of Jiangsu so that they can get to know each other's local economy better; it also provides as much as information as possible for Italian companies that might want to invest abroad, and has opened dedicated consultation offices to assist them. These visits have led to profitable results, as witnessed by the implementation of over 70 investment schemes in the province in just over a year, and 384 Italian firms have already relocated in part to China, with an overall investment of $1.6 billion.[11] The companies involved are mainly large ones, such as Fiat, Iveco, Brenda, Pirelli and Merloni MTS, but the number of small- and medium-sized enterprises is also on the rise. Fiat has made the biggest Italian investment in China, to the tune of around $1 billion and gained an ever-increasing share of the internal automotive market. Another important trade agreement achieved in this province involved setting up the Naveco joint venture, arising from the agreement between Iveco, a Fiat Group company, and the Nanjing Automotive Corporation. It has already made an important acquisition, namely the Yuejin Motors Company, establishing itself as one of the leaders in China's commercial vehicle market for mass transport with a production volume of about 70,000 commercial vehicles per year.

[10]Nanking Dossier at www.governo.it.

[11]Italy–China Dossier at www.governo.it.

7.2.2 The Agreement with the Guangdong Province

The mission led by the then Prime Minister, Romano Prodi, in September 2006, consisted of a large Italian delegation of over 500 firms, 26 industry associations, and 20 banks with delegations from ICE, Confindustria, and Italian regions and towns. The idea was to launch an Italian strategy aimed not only at learning more about their markets and undertaking new economic agreements to further improve their economic relationship but also at encouraging Chinese investment in Italy.

There were three main stages involved: the first in Nanking, to further consolidate economic relations with the province of Jiangsu and create new investment projects; the second in Canton, in the province of Guangdong (see Maps 7.3 and 7.4), with the aim of drawing up new agreements and encouraging the progress of small- and medium-sized enterprises in this market too; and the third in Shanghai in order to take part in EXPO 2010.

The most important outcome of this mission was achieved in Canton, where Confindustria and the Guangdong government signed a cooperation agreement, similar to that with Jiangsu province and with the aim of increasing both economic cooperation between the parties and reciprocal investment. This province, mainly characterized by small and medium-sized enterprises, was growing at a steady rate at that time, covering 14% of domestic GDP. It offered Italy many business opportunities in the sectors of communication, textiles, electronics and industrial machinery, all strong points in its rapid growth of around 30% a year (Cristaldi 2006a, b).

Map 7.3 Province of Guangdong, reprocessing by Augusto Frascatani, Department Memotef Sapienza University of Rome

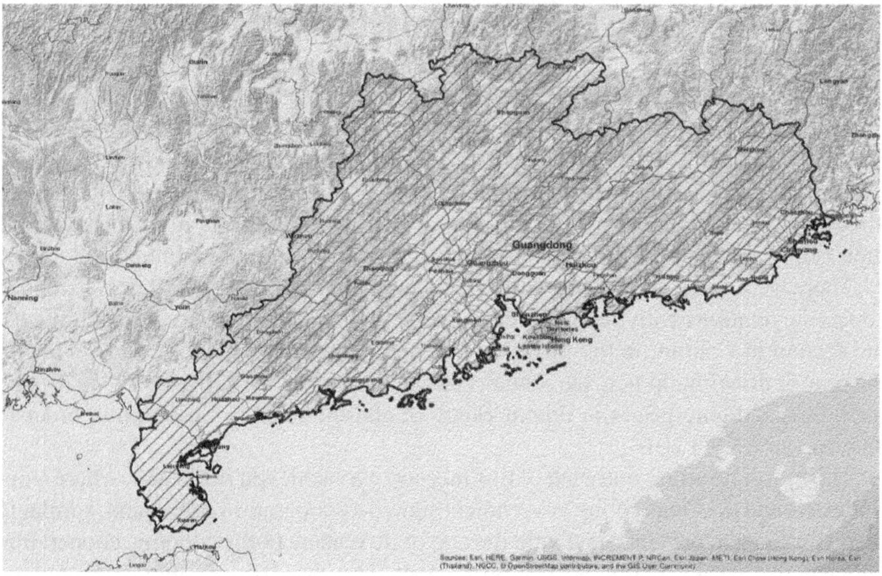

Map 7.4 Province of Guangdong, reprocessing by Augusto Frascatani, Department Memotef Sapienza University of Rome

The institutional agreement was designed to favour access for small- and medium-sized Italian enterprises by means of multisectoral support for all dynamic companies keen to accept new challenges abroad.

Italian firms therefore created new opportunities for entering the Chinese business world, with the chance to meet and mix with the dynamism of young local Chinese entrepreneurs with small, private firms; they are similar to Italian entrepreneurs, but with different experiences and qualities. This was an advantage for small- and medium-sized Chinese enterprises thanks to the creativity, industrial know-how, and the strength of the brands that led "Made in Italy" firms to strengthen cooperation and trade relations between the two countries.

This agreement helped Italy to significantly reduce the disparity with the other European countries in terms of investment, and it presented itself as both a bridge to connect China and Europe, and a doorway into Europe for Chinese goods and direct investment in Europe, thanks to its position in the Mediterranean area.

7.2.3 New Investment Prospects: The National Parks

Nowadays there are over 1400 firms present in China, 75% of which belong to big national groups and with only a small percentage of SMEs overall. They are mainly concentrated in the provinces of Jiangsu and Guangdong, and in Shanghai, where a total of about 60% of all the Italian firms have relocated, attracted by the presence of equipped areas and better competitiveness despite the cost of setting up being slightly higher than in other areas, while Peking was preferred for representations and institutional offices.

Some analyses of the sector, requested by the Ministry for Foreign affairs and by the Italian Embassy,[12] produced a detailed study of the industrial situation in China that identified the best and most favourable areas for setting up Italian businesses and investment.

The study highlights the great potential of the business area known as the "Pearl River Delta", located on the southern coast, and the situation relating to the industrial parks which are thriving all over China. The first area is located in the economic triangle formed by the cities of Canton, Shenzhen and Zhuhai, where thousands of Chinese and foreign companies are concentrated in a relatively small area of 40,000 km^2, which alone account for one-third of total annual exports and receive some 35% of the sum of foreign direct investment in China, thanks to the privileged policy for Shenzhen, which is one of the special economic areas. This area, where the electronics, watches, plastic and the automotive industry sectors are achieving excellence,[13] is characterized not only by low labour costs but also by a high level of specialization, qualified personnel and the abundance of raw materials, factors which make this area the most suitable for those wishing to invest in these sectors.

The industrial parks are the other factor in the Chinese economy that has enabled its growth in recent years. An estimate from 2004 counted 174 parks recognized at state level plus the countless parks promoted by the local authorities, distributed over three key areas: the Pearl River Delta; the Yangtze River Delta around Shanghai and the Bohai Bay Economic Rim formed by the cities of Peking, Tianjin and Dalian (Fig. 7.10). According to various criteria, such as the degree of development, the level of specialization, the availability of services, human resources, competitiveness, and the logistical position, a list has been drawn up of the 40 main industrial parks that are most favourable and suitable for setting up activities that are of interest to Italian SMEs in the car and car components, engineering, chemical, textile, pharmaceutical, furniture and agro-industry sectors. The park with the best overall characteristics for covering all sectors is the Tianjin Economic and Technological Development Zone (ETDZ), where local government incentives to favour investment seek to restore the city as the economic capital of the north. This is followed by the two parks in Shanghai: the Jinshan Industrial Park and the Zhangjiang High Tech; the former specializes in the automotive sector[14] and in machine tools, and the latter in biotechnology and pharmaceuticals. They are both favoured by Shanghai's excellent infrastructure and the presence of airports and international ports which provide connections all over the world.

---

[12]Studio Ambrosetti—The European House, March 2006.

[13]Sector that produces car parts and components.

[14]Historical Archive Bank of Italy, Carte De 'Stefani, 28, fasc. 6, newspaper clippings, "Il Sole. Giornale del Commercio, dell'Industria, del Finanza e dell'Agricoltura", Thursday 4 February 1937, a. XV.

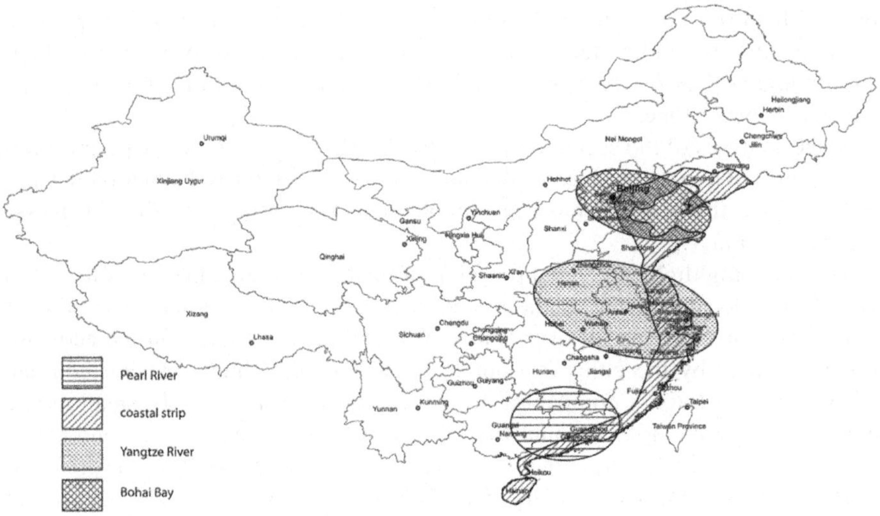

Fig. 7.10 Main economic areas. *Source* Reprocessing by data from the Ambrosetti Studio (made Augusto Frascatani, Department Memotef Sapienza University of Rome)

Finally, in the southern area, there is the Guangzhou ETDZ Park, which specializes in the furniture and furnishings sector with excellent growth prospects, also thanks to its proximity to Hong Kong and the presence of many foreign companies (Fig. 7.11).

Fig. 7.11 Main industrial parks. *Source* Reprocessing by data from the Ambrosetti Studio (made Augusto Frascatani, Department Memotef Sapienza University of Rome)

Chapter 8
Final Remarks

Investment Target Areas Prospects for Italy China

Abstract In this work we focused on the long-term trade relations between Italy and China to try to reconstruct and understand the commercial and economic interests of two countries that today, in this period of systemic globalization, are increasingly involved in a context where China more than others, over the last quarter of a century, has experienced an improvement in the quality of life of most of its population. It has also seen a remarkable development of its regions and coastal metropolises, an increase in international trade and the expansion of the range of exports, together with the ability to withstand external shocks. Despite the rigidity of the Chinese political system, where the communist party has retained a monopoly on power, it has also shown a great capacity for adaptation. Italy's penetration of China during the Belle Époque, and both before and between the two World Wars, though greater in numerical terms than in previous years, remained extremely modest when compared with the trade exchange that China already had with other European and non-European countries. On an economic level, various schemes for cooperation were attempted but never achieved the desired results. There were various reasons for these failures. Nevertheless, trade relations between Italy and China are an interesting case for illustrating the complexity of international dynamics. The absence of diplomatic relations between the two countries was actually counterbalanced by a reciprocal interest, seen in the development, albeit partial, of significant relations, though to a lesser extent compared with the other European countries. These contacts and this interest would lay the foundations for the diplomatic revolution in 1970 which in turn would lead to great changes. After the painful period of the Second World War and the political and economic changes in Italy and China, trade relations between the two countries strengthened and, given the trade trends and the trade agreements analysed, it can be broadly assumed that economic relations between Italy and China will become even closer, with plenty of room for further development, and stronger, with a positive influence on their future political and diplomatic relations. the growing commercial understanding is a further source of support for large-scale co-operative schemes, and not only in the economic sphere, where we find the memorandum signed by the Ministry for Foreign affairs and the National Development and Reform Commission of the People's Republic of China on the "financial cooperation to support the development of small and medium-sized enterprises and the setting up of a bilateral working group in this sector". Trade relations between Italy and China are continuously being

D. Strangio, *Italy-China Trade Relations*, Studies in Economic History,
https://doi.org/10.1007/978-3-030-39084-6_8

strengthened thanks, also, to different cultural initiatives. Ultimately, Italy is moving closer to China and the initiatives undertaken are seeking the secure establishment of Italian firms on the Chinese market; this policy offers ample possibilities for successful Italian investment and much more besides.

The role of foreign trade has been at the centre of the debate on economic policy since the 1970s. Trade policy has been the subject of various debates between supporters of liberalism and protectionism. The debate continued, albeit to a lesser extent, in the period between the two wars and resumed vigorously in the second post-war period, in the renewed interest in the problems of Italian economic growth in the long run and the fact that it lagged behind its European counterparts. A detailed analysis of this literature can be found in Cohen and Federico (2001). Here it is sufficient to recall two main strands: the first deals directly with the discussion on customs policy and the impact of the various measures. It can be traced to the controversial arguments of Gerschenkron (1962) against the duty on wheat and the tariff of 1887. Gerschenkron's criticisms were shared more recently by Fenoaltea (2006), who emphasizes above all the negative effect of the duty on wheat on the potential competitiveness of Italian industry. The policy was instead defended, though somewhat cautiously, by Zamagni (1993: 154–156). Federico (Federico and Tena 1998; Federico and O'Rourke 2000) argued, instead, that the level of protection was relatively low and therefore so was the overall effect of the modest customs policy. The second line of analysis focuses on the macroeconomic effects of openness to international trade. According to Bonelli (1979) and Cafagna (1989), the worldwide demand for primary products (especially silk) played an essential role as a stimulus for the start of economic development. Fenoaltea (2006) shares the idea of the propulsive role of openness to the international economy in the long term, but shifts his attention to twenty-year fluctuations (the "Kuznets cycle"). In this model, the supply of capital on the international market has determined the alternation, in the peripheral countries, including Italy, of periods of boom (and growth of trade) and stagnation. These hypotheses have so far been only subjected to partial verification, as a somewhat paradoxical consequence of the abundance of data on foreign trade.

In this work, we focused on the long-term trade relations between Italy and China to try to reconstruct and understand the commercial and economic interests of two countries that today, in this period of systemic globalization, are increasingly involved in a context where China more than others, over the last quarter of a century, has experienced an improvement in the quality of life of most of its population. It has also seen a remarkable development of its regions and coastal metropolises, an increase in international trade and the expansion of the range of exports, together with the ability to withstand external shocks. Despite the rigidity of the Chinese political system, where the communist party has retained a monopoly on power, it has also shown a great capacity for adaptation. The situation of the public finances is not safe from the risk of crises, and public debt is still moderate but is increasing rapidly and to this must be added the costs of restructuring the banking system and the implied debt of the social security system. Equally important for its international image (although there is still much to do) and the internal evolution of the political system is the progressive affirmation of the rule of law (Lemoine 2005, pp. 135–136). Italy's penetration of China during the Belle Époque, and both before and between the two world wars, though greater in numerical terms than in previous years, remained extremely modest when compared with the trade exchange that China already had with other European and non-European countries.

Italian policy towards China at that time displayed the same characteristics of uncertainty, contradiction and faintheartedness that marked the Italian government's foreign policy overall. Above all, policymakers were unable to grasp the mismatch between the goals to be pursued and the resources available; they were under the illusion that Italy could provide military aid, thereby guaranteeing a policy of neutrality between China and Japan, another emerging country in that part of the world (Borsa 1994, 288).

On an economic level, various schemes for cooperation were attempted but never achieved the desired results. There were various reasons for these failures: lack of capital, Italian entrepreneurs not being used to operating in a competitive regime, the backwardness of Italian industry compared with other European countries present in China at that time, inefficiency in the organization of its diplomatic representations, and a reluctance to grant deferred payments.

In China too there was no real commitment to creating a profitable business relationship with Italy: Chang Kai-Shek was only interested in receiving weapons and military assistance to fight the communists, and any schemes for economic cooperation were only useful for attracting international capital in order to block Japanese expansionism (Borsa 1994, pp. 289–290; Schmidt-Glintzer 2002, pp. 60–61). Nevertheless, trade relations between Italy and China are an interesting case for illustrating the complexity of international dynamics. The absence of diplomatic relations between the two countries was actually counterbalanced by a reciprocal interest, seen in the development, albeit partial, of significant relations, though to a lesser extent compared with the other European countries. These contacts and this interest would lay the foundations for the diplomatic revolution in 1970 which in turn would lead to great changes.

After the painful period of the Second World War and the political and economic changes in Italy and China, trade relations between the two countries strengthened and, given the trade trends and the trade agreements analysed, it can be broadly assumed that economic relations between Italy and China will become even closer, with plenty of room for further development, and stronger, with a positive influence on their future political and diplomatic relations. In addition, the growing commercial understanding is a further source of support for large-scale co-operative schemes, and not only in the economic sphere, where we find the memorandum signed by the Ministry for Foreign affairs and the National Development and Reform Commission of the People's Republic of China on the "financial cooperation to support the development of small and medium-sized enterprises and the setting up of a bilateral working group in this sector". For example, various public cooperation agreements[1]

[1] Italy–China Dossier, at www.governo.it.

have been arranged between the two governments which cover various sectors, estimated to be worth a total of €160 million: a credit line of €70 million has been allocated for projects for health and for the protection of cultural assets, while a memorandum on agriculture and the environment has provided for a grant of €80 million. Italy has taken part in some 57 projects for safeguarding the environment, which have been realized by means of co-financing to the tune of over €100 million. There has also been progress in cooperation between universities, and a joint campus for engineering and management was inaugurated in Shanghai with the participation of four universities, including the Bocconi in Milan and Luiss-Guido Carli in Rome, and the Fudan and Tongji universities in Shanghai. There are other projects with the Sapienza University in Rome in relation to International Credits Mobility and various bilateral agreements; furthermore, Italy's university system is working hard to attract and welcome more Chinese students and researchers, creating scholarships and exchange programmes to provide greater opportunities for the two cultures to be in direct contact and further strengthen their ties.

Some technical obstacles to their economic relations have yet to be resolved and could slow them down; some issues still remain open regarding the application of duties and different ways to protect the internal market on both sides (as illustrated by the ongoing disputes between the EU and China). Membership of the WTO has also caused China to standardize the rules for international business, especially from a legislative point of view, such as the protection of investment, protection of copyright and greater control over counterfeiting, areas on which China is working in order to achieve a total and complete liberalization of the markets as planned (Orlandi 2001; 2006).[2]

On 27 August 2018, a series of posts was begun on the Canton Consulate's Facebook page, dedicated to Italians in southern China who have distinguished themselves in some way, in particular Cristiano Varotti, who arrived in Changsha (capital of the Hunan region) in 2011 to manage the representation office of the Marche region (the two territories have a twinning agreement). He has stayed on in this region, where there are very few Italian residents, and has launched a wide range of consulting activities in order to establish institutional relations and promote business development for Italian and Chinese firms. In 2013, he founded the Meilin Consulting Company and was appointed as the representative for international relations in the Province of Hunan. He has been working for some years with Huayi Brothers Film and Culture City to create an Italian city in Changsha. In September 2018, "Casa Marche" was inaugurated, an area of 360 m^2 inspired by the region and its products and located inside "HB Italian Town", the theme park dedicated to tourism and to high-quality Italian products. It was built in Changsha and is a full-scale Italian village with lots

[2]The negotiations lasted 15 years. The WTO was born from the agreement signed in 1994 by 125 countries, which had gathered in Marrakesh in Morocco. This agreement was an attempt to modernize some of the economies in society as a whole. It also coincided with a period of sharp decline in the price of oil on international markets, which pushed countries like Saudi Arabia and Oman into the organization, in an attempt to help diversify their economies which were still dominated by oil and its derivatives (Parenti 2002, pp. 42–43; Farah 2005). See also Vinciguerra (2006a, b, c, d).

of restaurants, hotels, cinemas, theatres, shops and replicas of historical buildings. This project expects one and a half million visitors in the first year and five million by the end of the third year.

Trade relations between Italy and China are continuously being strengthened thanks to these cultural initiatives. As Portfiliu has written: "Increasingly, today's well-off Chinese public has been demanding that reports be made accessible, and in recent years this has also been promoted by the government, as is well reflected in a State Council document which states: "it is significant to give life to those collections in the museums, to the vast lands, and to words in ancient books, to the inheritance of Chinese traditional culture, to the satisfaction of public cultural demand, to the enhancement of population cohesion, and to boost social and economic development" (State Council 2016). For example, a new form of heritage interpretation and utilization, the National Archaeological Site Parks (NASPs) has been officially designated/inaugurated? by the SACH. Up to the present time, a total of 36 NASPs have been announced in 2010, 2013 and 2018. The Guidelines for Historic Buildings Open to the Public in 2017 (SACH 2017) have been published, in which various forms of accessibility are encouraged for historic buildings occupied by governments, public bodies, enterprises and individuals" (Porfyriou et al. 2018, p. 30).

Ultimately, Italy is moving closer to China and the initiatives undertaken are seeking the secure establishment of Italian firms on the Chinese market; this policy offers ample possibilities for successful Italian investment and much more besides.[3]

[3]Chinese President Xi Jinping, on an official visit to Rome in March 2019, signed the memorandum on the New Silk Road with Prime Minister Giuseppe Conte. Twenty-nine institutional and commercial agreements have been signed between Italy and China. Called the Belt and Road Initiative (BRI) in English, the New Silk Road is a strategic initiative designed by China to "improve its trade links with the Eurasian countries". In detail, it would mean the development of a whole series of transport and logistics infrastructures, through land connections (especially railways) and maritime ones for a total of six large corridors, which would further connect China to Central Asia and Europe. The New Silk Road project was born in 2013 thanks to Chinese President Xi Jinping, with Beijing putting up the $1000 billion to be spent on investments (see Fig. A.1 in Appendix).

Appendix

See Table A.1 and Fig. A.1.

Table A.1 Exports–Imports data: Italy towards China (1970–2016) (millions of euros-eurolire until 1998)

Years	Exports	Imports	Balances (Exports–Imports)
1970	18	20	−2
1971	19	21	−2
1972	23	25	−2
1973	22	39	−17
1974	35	39	−4
1975	49	44	5
1976	59	68	−9
1977	40	74	−34
1978	83	90	−7
1979	120	169	−49
1980	114	193	−79
1981	190	234	−44
1982	146	298	−152
1983	208	325	−117
1984	408	395	13
1985	778	579	199
1986	772	525	247
1987	730	686	44
1988	873	962	−89
1989	877	1.195	−318
1990	603	1.132	−529
1991	803	1.458	−655
1992	951	1.765	−814

(continued)

D. Strangio, *Italy-China Trade Relations*, Studies in Economic History,
https://doi.org/10.1007/978-3-030-39084-6

Table A.1 (continued)

Years	Exports	Imports	Balances (Exports–Imports)
1993	2.006	2.104	−98
1994	1.898	2.596	−698
1995	2.267	3.298	−1.031
1996	2.285	3.215	−930
1997	2.224	3.881	−1.657
1998	1.842	4.342	−2.500
1999	1.834	5.001	−3.167
2000	2.380	7.028	−4.648
2001	3.275	7.484	−4.209
2002	4.017	8.307	−4.290
2003	3.850	9.553	−5.703
2004	4.448	11.828	−7.380
2005	4.605	14.131	−9.526
2006	5.685	17.910	12.225
2007	6.289	21.689	15.399
2008	6.432	23.606	17.173
2009	6.629	19.333	12.704
2010	8.608	28.788	20.179
2011	9.995	29.573	19.577
2012	8.998	25.006	16.007
2013	9.842	23.070	13.227
2014	10.493	25.075	14.581
2015	10.412	28.232	17.819
2016	11.057	27.345	16.288

Source Database ITAT www.coeweb.istat.it

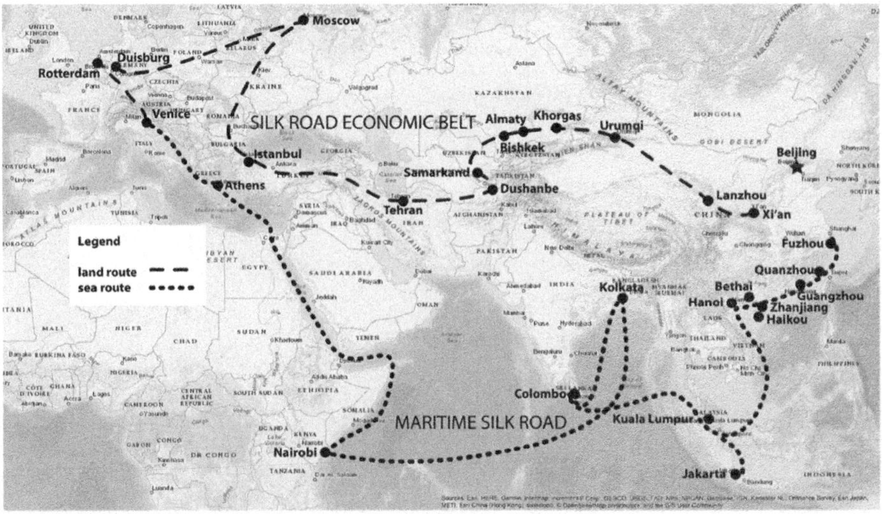

Fig. A.1 Silk Road Economic belt and Maritime Silk Road. Reprocessing by Augusto Frascatani, Department Memotef Sapienza University of Rome

Sources

Historical Archive Bank of Italy

Historical Archive Bank of Italy, Carte De 'Stefani, 28, fasc. 6, newspaper clippings, "Il Sole. Giornale del Commercio, dell'Industria, del Finanza e dell'Agricoltura", Thursday 4 February 1937, a. XV.

Historical Archive Bank of Italy, Carte De Stefani, 30, fasc. 1 *Lettera di Alberto De' Stefani al Generalissimo dopo avere lasciato la Cina.*

Historical Diplomatic Archives of the Ministry of Foreign Affairs, Ministry of Foreign Affairs Writings: Kingdom of Italy 1861–1887—*Mission of the Cav. Cristoforo Negri to establish a diplomatic representation in Japan and China (April–July 1863)*

Historical Diplomatic Archives of the Ministry of Foreign Affairs, Ministry of Foreign Affairs Writings: Kingdom of Italy 1861–1887, Busta 18 Fascicolo 7, Letter from Cav. Cristoforo Negri to the Ministry's Secretary General, Turin 5 February 1863.

Historical Diplomatic Archives of the Ministry of Foreign Affairs, Ministry of Foreign Affairs Writings: Kingdom of Italy 1861–1887, Busta 18, Fascicolo 7, Letter from the engineer Sibaldi to the Foreign Minister for the Kingdom of Italy, Florence 27 June 1863.

Historical Diplomatic Archives of the Ministry of Foreign Affairs, Ministry of Foreign Affairs Writings: Kingdom of Italy 1861–1887, Busta 18, Fascicolo 7, Ministry of the Navy, Cabinet of the Minister, No. 1497, Subject: Mission in China, Turin, 17 May 1863.

Historical Diplomatic Archives of the Ministry of Foreign Affairs, Ministry of Foreign Affairs Political Series Inventory A. 1888–1891

Historical Diplomatic Archives of the Ministry of Foreign Affairs, Ministry of Foreign Affairs Political Series Inventory A. 1888–1891, Busta 22, Fascicolo 7, *Protection in China of Italian Missionaries (1888–1890),* Letter of the Royal Minister in Shanghai to the Ministry of Foreign Affairs, No. 1112, Subject: New phase of the dispute over French passports to missionaries in China, Shanghai June 29, 1887.

D. Strangio, *Italy-China Trade Relations*, Studies in Economic History,
https://doi.org/10.1007/978-3-030-39084-6

Historical Diplomatic Archives of the Ministry of Foreign Affairs, Ministry of Foreign Affairs Political Series Inventory A. 1888–1891, Busta 22, Fascicolo 7, *Protection in China of Italian Missionaries (1888–1890),* directed memorandum from the Royal Legation in China to Tsung-li Yamen, Shanghai 5 June 1888.

Historical Diplomatic Archives of the Ministry of Foreign Affairs, Ministry of Foreign Affairs Political Series Inventory A. 1888–1891, Busta 22, Fascicolo 7, *Protection in China of Italian Missionaries (1888–1890)*, Letter from Ferdinando De Luca to His Excellency the Minister of State for Foreign Affairs, n.general 71, report 43, Answer to letter April Div. 1Sez. 1, 10749/1b, Shanghai 5 June, 1888.

Historical Diplomatic Archives of the Ministry of Foreign Affairs, Ministry of Foreign Affairs Political Series Inventory A. 1888–1891, Busta 22, Fascicolo 7, *Protection in China of Italian Missionaries (1888–1890)*, Legation of His Majesty the King of Italy in China, general No. 179—report no. 116, Shanghai 31 October 1888.

Historical Diplomatic Archives of the Ministry of Foreign Affairs, Political Series Inventory. A 1888–1891, Letter from the Minister of Foreign Affairs Tittoni to Carlo Baroli, Rome 16 January 1905.

Historical Diplomatic Archives of the Ministry of Foreign Affairs, Political Series Inventory. A 1888–1891, Busta 22—Fascicolo 7, Legation of H. M. the King of Italy in China, Letter from the Prince of Cariati, Beijing 16 December 1889.

Historical Diplomatic Archives of the Ministry of Foreign Affairs, Political Series Inventory. A 1888–1891, Busta 22—Fascicolo 7, Legation of H.M. the King of Italy in China, Beijing 25 August 1890.

Historical Diplomatic Archives of the Ministry of Foreign Affairs, Political Series Inventory. A 1888–1891, Busta 22—Fascicolo 7, Legation of H. M. the King of Italy in China, Beijing 10 March 1890.

Historical Diplomatic Archives of the Ministry of Foreign Affairs, Political Series Inventory. A 1888–1891, Busta 22—Fascicolo 7, Legation of H.M. the King of Italy in Shanghai, Shanghai 8 November 1889.

Historical Diplomatic Archives of the Ministry of Foreign Affairs, Political Series Inventory. A 1888–1891, Busta 22—Fascicolo 7, Legation of H.M. the King of Italy in Shanghai, Shanghai 28 December, 1890.

Historical Diplomatic Archives of the Ministry of Foreign Affairs, Political Series Inventory. A 1888–1891, Busta 22—Fascicolo 7, Letter from the Regent of the Consulate Ernesto Ghisi, Subject: experiment to export mineral water from Italy, Shanghai 11 September 1890.

Historical Diplomatic Archives of the Ministry of Foreign Affairs, Political Series Inventory. A 1888–1891, Extract from a letter of the Prince of Cariati, Shanghai 10 June 1888.

Historical Diplomatic Archives of the Ministry of Foreign Affairs, Political Series P 1891–1916

Historical Diplomatic Archives of the Ministry of Foreign Affairs Political Series Inventory P 1891–1916, Letter by His Excellency the Hon. Grinetti from the Royal legation in Tokyo, Subject: rumours of new paperwork for the concessions of San Mun, Tokyo 24 April 1902.

Historical Diplomatic Archives of the Ministry of Foreign Affairs, Political Series P. 1891–1916, Pacco 422, Posizione 86/3 *Arms sales in China*, Letter from Dr. Eugenio Donegani to His Excellency Mr Nitti, The Minister of Agriculture, Industry and Commerce, Beijing 7 November 1911.
Historical Diplomatic Archives of the Ministry of Foreign Affairs, Political Series P 1891–1916, Pacco 511, *Purchase and construction of warships,* Legation of H. M. the King of Italy in China, No. 833/249, Letter from Livio Borghese to His Excellency Senator T. Tittoni, the Minister for Foreign Affairs, Beijing 30 December, 1907.
Historical Diplomatic Archives of the Ministry of Foreign Affairs, Political Series P 1891–1916, Letter from His Excellency the Marquis of San Giuliano to Count Sforza, No. 747/207, Subject: possible sale of Italian sales.
Historical Diplomatic Archives of the Ministry of Foreign Affairs, Political Series Inventory P 1891–1916, Pacco 511, *Purchase and construction of warships,* Legation of H.M. the King of Italy in China, No. 74/18, Letter from Livio Borghese to His Excellency Senator T. Tittoni, the Minister of Foreign Affairs, Beijing 25 January 1908.
Historical Diplomatic Archives of the Ministry of Foreign Affairs, Political Series P 1891–1916, Pacco 511, *Purchase and construction of warships,* The Chinese army on 1 March, 1910, Bulletin No. 15 of the Italian Military Staff Corps Command, Colonial Office.

Historical Diplomatic Archives of the Ministry of Foreign Affairs, Inventory of Political Affairs Series 1919–1930

Historical Diplomatic Archives of the Ministry of Foreign Affairs, Political Affairs Series Inventory 1919–1930, Pacco 950, *Italian Bank in China*, Letter of G. A. Bena, President of the Italian Chamber of Commerce in China, Shanghai, 20 October 1918, p. 9.
Historical Diplomatic Archives of the Ministry of Foreign Affairs, Political Affairs Series Inventory 1919–1930, Pacco 950, *Italian Bank in China* Letter of G. A. Bena, President of the Italian Chamber of Commerce in China, Shanghai, 20 October 1918, pp. 10–13.
Historical Diplomatic Archives of the Ministry of Foreign Affairs, Political Affairs Series Inventory 1919–1930, Pacco 950, *Italian Bank in China*, Letter of the Real Legation in Beijing No. 101/13, Beijing 25 January 1919.
Historical Diplomatic Archives of the Ministry of Foreign Affairs, Political Affairs Series Inventory 1919–1930, Pacco 951, Fascicolo 2057 bis, Letter from the Royal Italian Legation to S. E. Count Sforza, Minister of Foreign Affairs, Beijing July 29, 1920, pp. 1–3.
Historical Diplomatic Archives of the Ministry of Foreign Affairs, Political Affairs Series Inventory 1919–1930, Pacco 951, Fascicolo 2057 bis, Letter of the Royal Italian Legation to S. E. Conte Sforza, Minister of Foreign Affairs, Beijing July 29, 1920, p. 4.
Historical Diplomatic Archives of the Ministry of Foreign Affairs, Political Affairs Series Inventory 1919–1930, Pacco 951, Fascicolo 2057 bis, Ministry of War-General Directorates of Artillery, Subject: Arms sales to China, Rome March 1921.

Historical Diplomatic Archives of the Ministry of Foreign Affairs, Political Affairs Series Inventory 1919–1930, Pacco 951, Fascicolo 2057 bis, Letter of G. A. Bena, President of the Italian Chamber of Commerce in China, Shanghai 20 October 1918. pp. 3–8.
Historical Diplomatic Archives of the Ministry of Foreign Affairs, Political Affairs Series Inventory 1919–1930, Pacco 953, Fascicolo 2087, *Customs Conference*, Letter from Dr. T. Cerruti No. 296-93, Beijing March 28, 1924.
Historical Diplomatic Archives of the Ministry of Foreign Affairs, Political Affairs Series Inventory 1919–1930, Pacco 953, Fascicolo 2087, *Custom Conference*, Telegram incoming No. 3635 of the R. Minister in Beijing to the Minister of Foreign Affairs, Subject: Customs Conference, Beijing 5 November 1925.
Historical Diplomatic Archives of the Ministry of Foreign Affairs, Political Affairs Series Inventory 1919–1930, Pacco 953, Fascicolo 2087, *Custom Conference,* Letter from the Italian Bank in China and the Trieste Shipyard to the Ministry of Foreign Affairs, Rome 4 January 1927.
Historical Diplomatic Archives of the Ministry of Foreign Affairs, Political Affairs Series Inventory 1919-1930, Pacco 962, Fascicolo 2143, The Chinese customs issue, Camillo Fumagalli, s.d. p. 1
Historical Diplomatic Archives of the Ministry of Foreign Affairs, Political Affairs Series Inventory 1919–1930, Pacco 962, Fascicolo 2143, *Custom Conference—Chinese surcharge rates,* Letter to S. E Minister of Foreign Affairs, No. 2694/99, Subject: Illegal surtaxes of the government of Nanjing, Shanghai, September 14, 1927.
Historical Diplomatic Archives of the Ministry of Foreign Affairs, Political Affairs Series Inventory 1919–1930, Pacco 965, Fascicoli 2155 and 2155bis, Letter of the Italian Legation, No. 1147/204, Pos. A.18, Subject: Mission to Nanjing for new treaty (report of the negotiation), Beijing 3 december 1928, Year VII Fascist Era.
Historical Diplomatic Archives of the Ministry of Foreign Affairs, Inventory Series Political Affairs 1919–1930, Pacco 965, Fascicoli 2155 and 2155bis, Rome Agency—Daily Information Bulletin No. 291, The Italian-Chinese Treaty and Italian Interests, Rome Thursday 6 December 1928, Year VII Fascist Era.
Historical Diplomatic Archives of the Ministry of Foreign Affairs, Inventory of Political Affairs Series 1919–1930, Pacco 965, Fascicoli 2155 and 2155bis, R. Legation Beijing, Annex A to Report No. 864/147, 24 August 1928.
Historical Archives of the Ministry of Foreign Affairs, Political Affairs Series Inventory 1919–1930, Pacco 965, Fascicoli 2155 and 2155bis, Royal Legation Beijing, Annex B of Report No. ° 864/147, 24 August 1928.

Historical Diplomatic Archives of the Ministry of Foreign Affairs, Archive of Commerce 1919–1923

Historical Diplomatic Archives of the Ministry of Foreign Affairs, Archive of Commerce 1919–1923, Classi 5–7, Letter from the Italian Consulate to the R. Ministry of Foreign Affairs, no. 408-n. Spec 45-pos. 12, Object: Italian trade in China in 1922, Hong Kong 18 June 1923, p. 1.
Historical Diplomatic Archives of the Ministry of Foreign Affairs, Political Affairs Series Inventory 1919–1930, Classi 5–7, Letter from the Italian Consulate to the

R. Ministry of Foreign Affairs, no. 408-n. Spec 45-pos. 12, Object: Italian trade in China in 1922, Hong Kong 18 June 1923, pp. 3–7.

Historical Diplomatic Archives of the Ministry of Foreign Affairs, Archive of Commerce 1924–1926

Historical Diplomatic Archives of the Ministry of Foreign Affairs, Archive of Commerce 1924–1926, Classi 1–27, Letter of the Real Consulate of Italy to S. E. Hon. Benito Mussolini, Minister of Foreign Affairs, Tientsin, 23 May 1924.
Historical Diplomatic Archives of the Ministry of Foreign Affairs, Archive of Commerce 1924–1926, Classi 28–52, Reminder: Interesting issues Italy during negotiations with China, Beijing 10 December 1924.
Historical Diplomatic Archives of the Ministry of Foreign Affairs, Archive of Commerce 1924–1926, Classi 28–52, Italian Concession in Tientsin, Basic Regulation, pp. 3–6.
Historical Diplomatic Archives of the Ministry of Foreign Affairs, Archive of Commerce 1924–1926, Classi 28–52, Italian Concession in Tientsin, Regulation for Cleanliness and hygiene, pp. 7–11.
Historical Diplomatic Archives of the Ministry of Foreign Affairs, Archive of Commerce, 1924–1926, Classi 28–52, Italian Concession in Tientsin, Tax table, pp. 17–18.

Sitography

http://it.chinabroadcast.cn.
www.governo.it/governoinforma/dossier/cina.
www.valuepartnersgroup.com.
www.ilsole24ore.com.
www.esteri.it/coordinamentocina.
http://it.chineseembassy.org.
www.ecic.net/italian/associazione.
www.cinaoggi.it.
www.worldbank.org.
www.istat.it.
www.associna.com.
www.confindustria.it.
www.ice.gov.it.
www.italiacina.org.
www.sanpaoloimprese.com.
www.tuttocina.it.
www.cina.sanpaoloimprese.com.
www.esteri.it/doc/parchi.pdf, "*Prospezioni di mercato e studio dei parchi cinesi*", a cura di Studio Ambrosetti –The European House, Marzo '06.
www.governo.it (Dossier Italia-Cina; Dossier Nanchino).
Bertolozzi, D. 2006. Sul declinante celeste impero piomba il colonialismo europeo. http://www.storiain.net/artic/artic2.asp. luglio-agosto.
Michielin, R., La rivolta dei Boxers. Un "fondamentalismo" cinese di 100 anni fa. http://www.cronologia.it/storia/mondiale/cina008.htm.
ISTAT www.coeweb.istat.it.
https://www.ice.it/it/sites/default/files/inline-files/83c%20Scheda%20Paese%20Cina%20aggiornamento%20luglio%202018.pdf (scheda Cina Farnesina 2018).
https://www.coeweb.istat.it/serie_storiche.asp?mese=-1&flusso1=ON&flusso2=ON&riga=ANNO&gruppo=S_PAESE.
https://www.coeweb.istat.it/run/serie_storiche_run.asp?TRASPOSTA=&TITOLO_TABELLA=Serie+storica+%28Import%29+per+Paesi&GRUPPO=S_PAESE&

D. Strangio, *Italy-China Trade Relations*, Studies in Economic History,
https://doi.org/10.1007/978-3-030-39084-6

FLUSSO=8&TIPO_VALORE=M&RIGA=S_PAESE&VARIABILE=VALORE&PERIODICITA=A&ANNOA=2016&ANNO=2006&VALUTA=Euro&button1=Esegui.
Mercati esteri: http://www.infomercatiesteri.it/scambi_commerciali.php?id_paesi=122.

Bibliography

Benigno, Francesco. 2015. *La mala setta. Alle origini di mafia e camorra 1859–1878*. Turin: Einaudi.

Bertolozzi, D. 2006. Sul declinante celeste impero piomba il colonialismo europeo, luglio-agosto. http://www.storiain.net/artic/artic2.asp

Bin, Wong R. 1997. *China transformed: Historical change and the limits of European experience*. Ithaca and London: Cornell University Press.

Bof, Frediano. 2015. *Grande Guerra e primo Dopoguerra* (Chap. V, pp. 89–118), *Economia e politica economica in età fascista* (Chap. VI pp. 119–156), *Dalla guerra d'Africa alla seconda guerra mondiale* (Chap. VII, pp. 157–186) in *L'Italia economica. Tempi e fenomeni del Cambiamento* (1861–2000) ed. Paolo Pecorari, and Padova, Cedam.

Bonelli, Franco. 1979. Il capitalismo italiano: linee generali di interpretazione. In *Storia d'Italia. Annali*, I, *Dal feudalesimo al capitalismo*, 1195–1255. Turin: Einaudi.

Borsa, Giorgio. 1961. *Italia e Cina nel secolo XIX*. Milan: Edizioni di Comunità.

Borsa, Giorgio. 1969. La crisi italo-cinese del marzo 1899 nelle carte inedite del ministro Canevaro. *Il Politico* 34 (4): 618–644.

Borsa, Giorgio. 1977. *La nascita del mondo moderno in Asia orientale*. Milan: Rizzoli.

Borsa, Giorgio. 1994. *Europa e Asia tra modernità e tradizione*. Milan: FrancoAngeli.

Boulnois, L. 2005. *La via della seta. Dei guerrieri, mercanti*, Milan, Bompiani (tit.or. La route de la soie, Genéve Edition Oliane, 2001).

Brivio, E. 2006. Componenti auto: la UE contro i dazi di Pechino. In *Economia e Impresa*, *Il Sole 24 Ore*, 16 Sept.

Cafagna, Luciano. 1989. *Dualismo e sviluppo nella storia d'Italia*. Marsilio: Venice.

Capanna, A., and O. Messeri. 1940. *Gli scambi commerciali dell'Italia con l'estero dalla costituzione del Regno ad oggi*. Rome: Unione editorial d'Italia.

Carreras, Albert. 2002. Il XX secolo, tra rottura e prosperità. In *Dall'espansione allo sviluppo. Una storia economica d'Europa*, ed. Antonio Di Vittorio. Turin: G. Giappichelli.

Cavalcanti, Maria Luisa. 1984. *La politica commerciale italiana 1945–1952. Uomini e fatti*. Naples: Edizioni Scientifiche Italiane.

Cerretano, Valerio. 2004. The benefits of moderate inflation. The Rayon industry and Snia Viscosa in the Italy of the 1920s. *The Journal of the European Economic History*, 33, 2.

Cerretano, Valerio. 2018. Multinational business and hot countries in times of crisi: Courtauld, Glanzstoff, and Italy in the interwar period. *The Economic History Review* 71 (2): 540–566.

Checcoli, Ippolita (ed.). 2015. *I monti frumentari e le forme di credito non monetarie tra Medioevo ed Età contemporanea*. Bologna: Il Mulino.

Chen, Baoshun. 2000. "Ricordo del 30° anniversario delle relazioni diplomatiche tra Italia e Cina. In *Mondo Cinese* n°105, 71-74, Milan. Pubblicato da Istituto Italo-Cinese per gli scambi economici e culturali. https://www.tuttocina.it/Mondo_cinese/105/105_chen.htm.

D. Strangio, *Italy-China Trade Relations*, Studies in Economic History,
https://doi.org/10.1007/978-3-030-39084-6

Chiarlone, Stefano, and Alessia Amighini. 2007. *L'economia della Cina*. Rome, Carocci: Dalla pianificazione al mercato.

Chilosi, David, and Giovanni Federico. 2013. *Asian globalisations: Market integration, trade and economic growth, 1800–1938*, 1–87. Economic History Working Papers 54574, London School of Economics and Political Science, Department of Economic History.

Cipolletta, Innocenzo. 2006. Dal catenaccio al contropiede. In *Mondo e Mercati, Il Sole 24 Ore*, 12 Sept.

Coco, Orazio. 2016. Il colonialismo tedesco in Cina: L'isola di Qīngdǎo e la Baia di Jiāozhōu (1897–1914). In *Giornale di Storia*, vol. 20, 1–19. www.giornaledistoria.net.

Coco, Orazio. 2017a. Il nazionalismo cinese e il fascismo italiano: un decennio di cooperazione politica ed economica (1928–1937). In *Dimensioni e problemi della ricerca storica*, vol. 1, 185–214.

Coco, Orazio. 2017b. *Colonialismo europeo in Estremo Oriente: L'esperienza delle concessioni territoriali in Cina*. Rome: Nuova Cultura.

Coco, Orazio. 2019. Italian diplomacy in China: The forgotten affair of Sān Mén Xiàn (1898–1899). *Journal of Modern Italian Studies* 24 (2): 328–349.

Cohen, John, and Federico Giovanni. 2001. *The economic development of Italy* (trad. Ita. *Lo sviluppo economico italiano 1820–1960*, Bologna: Il Mulino). Cambridge: Cambridge University Press.

Conenna, Nadia, and Andrea Jacchia (eds.). 1988. *Tra politica e impresa: vita di Dino Gentili*, prefazione di Paolo Barile, biography of Giorgio Luti, testimonials by Antonio Alosco. Florence: Passigli.

Corradini, Piero. 1969. *La Cina*. Turin: Unione tipografico-editrice torinese.

Corradini, P. 1991a. Italia-Cina: dalle prime relazioni consolari al trattato di pace del 1947. In *Mondo Cinese* n. 76, Milan December, 7–49.

Corradini, Piero. 1991b. La concessione italiana di TienTsin. In *Mondo Cinese*, n. 75, September, 69–73. Milan.

Cristaldi, Sara. 2006a. Ice pioniere in Cina. In *Mondo e Mercati, Il Sole 24 Ore*, 12 Sept.

Cristaldi, Sara. 2006b, L'Italia adesso porta le pmi in Cina. In *Il sole 24 Ore*, 18 July, rassegna stampa: Value Partners.

Daniele, Vittorio, and Paolo Malanima. 2011. *Il Divario Nord-Sud in Italia 1861–2011*. Soveria Mannelli (CZ): Rubbettino.

De Antonellis, Giacomo. 1977. L'Italia in Cina nel XX secolo. In *Mondo Cinese* n°19, Milano Luglio, 51–55.

De Felice, Renzo. 2000. *Breve storia del fascismo*. Milan: Mondatori.

De Giorgi, Laura, and Guido Samarani. 2018. *Alberto De' Stefani: from Ca' Foscari to China, in 150 Years of Oriental Studies at Ca' Foscari*. ed Laura De Giorgi, and Federico Greselin, Ca Foscari (VE) I libri di Ca' Foscari 6, 163–171.

Di Martino, Paolo, and Michelangelo Vasta. 2017. *Ricchi per caso. La parabola dello sviluppo italiano*. Bologna: Il Mulino.

Eichengreen, Barry. 1994. Institutional prerequisites for economic growth: Europe after World War II. *European Economic Review* 38: 883–890.

Eichengreen, Barry. 2004. *Gabbie d'oro. Il «gold standard» e la grande depressione 1919–1939*. Bari: Cariplo-Laterza.

Eichengreen, Barry. 2007. *The European Economy since 1945: Coordinated capitalism and beyond*. Princeton: Princeton University Press (trad. Ita *La nascita dell'economia europea. Dalla svolta del 1945 alla sfida dell'innovazione* Milan, Il Saggiatore 2009).

Fairbanck, John K. 1988. *Storia della Cina contemporanea*. Milan: Rizzoli.

Fairbanck, J.K. 1988. *Storia della Cina contemporanea*. Milan: Rizzoli.

Farah, Paolo. 2005. L'adesione della Cina all'OMC: ovvero come conciliare cultura e diritto. In *Mondo Cinese* n.124, 34–42. Milan Luglio.

Fardella Enrico, and Prodi Giorgio. 2017. *The belt and road initiative impact on Europe: An italian perspective*. China World Economy

Favero, Giovanni. 2010. Le statistiche dei salari industriali in periodo fascista. *Quaderni storici* 134/a LXV(2): 2–40.

Federico, Giovanni. 1979. Per una analisi del ruolo dell'agricoltura nello sviluppo economico italiano: note sull'esportazione di prodotti primary (1863–1913). In *Società e Storia*, vol. 5, 379–441.

Federico, Giovanni. 1988. Commercio estero e "periferie". Il caso dei paesi mediterranei. *Meridiana* 4: 163–196.

Federico, Giovanni. 1994a. Agricoltura e sviluppo (1820–1950): verso una reinterpretazione? In *Il progresso economico dell'Italia*, ed. Pier Luigi Ciocca. Bologna: Il Mulino.

Federico, Giovanni. 1994b. *Il filo d'oro. L'industria mondiale della seta dalla trasformazione alla grande crisi*. Venice: Marsilio.

Federico, Giovanni, Giuseppe Tattara, and Michelangelo Vasta. 2011. Il Commercio estero italiano dall'Unificazione al 1939. In *Il Commercio estero italiano 1862–1950*, ed. Giovanni Federico, Sandra Natoli, Giuseppe Tattara, and Michelangelo Vasta, 3–50. Rome-Bari: Laterza.

Federico, Giovanni, and Tena Junguito, Antonio. 1998. Was Italy a protectionist country? *European Review of Economic History* 2: 73–97.

Federico, Giovanni, and O'Rourke Kevin. 2000. Much ado about nothing? The Italian trade policy in the 19th century. In *The Mediterranean response to globalisation before 1950*, ed. J. Williamson, and S. Pamuk (a cura di), 269–296. Routledge: London.

Felice, Emanuele. 2007. *Divari regionali e intervento pubblico. Per una rilettura dello sviluppo in Italia*. Bologna: Il Mulino.

Fenoaltea, Stefano. 2001. *La crescita industriale delle regioni d'Italia dall'Unità alla grande guerra: una prima stima per gli anni censuari*. Rome: Bank of Italy.

Fenoaltea, Stefano. 2006. *L'economia italiana dall'Unità alla Grande Guerra*. Laterza: Rome-Bari.

Findlay, Ronald, Kevin H. O'Rourke. 2007. *Power and plenty. Trade, war and the world economy in the second millennium*. Princeton: Princeton University Press.

Francioni, Andrea. 2004. *Il banchetto cinese. L'Italia fra le treaty powers*. Siena: NIE.

Francioni, Andrea. s.d. *Il trattato italo-cinese del 1866 nelle carte dell'Ammiraglio Arminjon, Siena*, 41–44. Dipartimento di Scienze Storiche, Giuridiche, Politiche e Sociali dell'Università degli studi di Siena.

Galor, Oded. 2011. *Unified growth theory*. Princeton: Princeton University Press.

Galor, Oded, and David N. Weil. 2000. Population, technology, and growth: From Malthusian stagnation to the demographic transition and beyond. *American Economic Review* 90 (4): 806–828.

Galor, Oded, and Omer Moav. 2004. From physical to human capital accumulation: Inequality and the process of development. *The Review of Economic Studies* 71 (4): 1001–1026.

Garofalo, Giuseppe. 1999. *Istituzioni di Economia politica—Macroeconomia di primo livello*, vol. 1. Turin: G. Giappichelli.

Gerschenkron, Alexander. 1965. *Il Problema storico dell'arretratezza economica*, Turin: Einaudi (Or. (1962), *Economic backwardness in historical perspective*, Cambridge, (Mass). Bellknap.

Giuntini, Andrea. 1991. *Leopoldo e il treno. Le ferrovie nel Granducato di Toscana 1824–1861*. Naples: Esi.

Giuntini, Andrea. 2001. *Il Paese che si muove. Le ferrovie in Italia fra '800 e '900*. Milan: Angeli.

ICE, Rapporto. 2006. *L'economia della Cina nel 2006*. www.ice.gov.it/estero2/cina. Italian Trade Commission Beijing office.

Lemoine, Françoise. 2005. *L'economia cinese*. Bologna: Il Mulino; Paris: La Découverte.

Luzzatto, Gino. 1968. *L'economia italiana dal 1861 al 1894*. Turin: Einaudi.

Maggi, Stefano. 2005. *Storia dei trasporti in Italia*. Bologna: Il Mulino.

Mancini, Claudio M. 1987. *Appunti per una storia delle relazioni commerciali e finanziarie tra Italia e Cina: dal 1814 al 1900* (Pt. 1). Milan: E.G.S.

Marcelli, Angelina. 2013. *Produzione serica, cultura contadina e politiche d'intervento pubblico in età contemporanea. Una storia nascosta. Il caso della Calabria*. Rome: Aracne.

Marroni, Carlo. 2006. Ora un'alleanza strategic. *Il Sole 24 Ore*, September 14.

Massimi, Silvia. 2000. La cooperazione italiana in Cina. In *Mondo Cinese*, n°104, 25–40. Milan: Maggio.

Meneguzzi Rostagni, Carla. 2012. Italia e Cina. Un secolo di relazioni. *Italogramma* 2: 43–53 (Identità italiana e civiltà globale all'inizio del ventunesimo secolo. http://italogramma.elte.hu).

Ministero degli Affari esteri e della Cooperazione internazionale. 1991. *I Documenti diplomatici italiani*. Serie ottava, (1935–1939) vol. II (1 September–31 December 1935). Rome: Istituto Poligrafico dello Stato.

Mondaini, Gennaro. 1927. *Manuale di storia e legislazione coloniale del regno d'Italia*. Rome: A. Sampolesi.

Montanelli, Indro. 2003a. *L'Italia in camicia nera*. Milan: RCS.

Montanelli, Indro. 2003b. *Introduzione, L'Italia dei notabili. Dal 1861 al 1900*, Milan: RCS quotidiani.

Orlandi, M. 2016. *Il commercio internazionale e la sua regolamentazione: una storia dei Trattati economici e commerciali*, Collana Saggi di teoria generale dello Stato e della finanza pubblica, diretta dal prof. Pietro Boria e dal prof. Alfonso Celotto, Wolters Kluwer, Padova, Cedam.

Orlandi, Romeo. 2001, L'adesione della Cina al WTO. In *Mondo Cinese* n°108, 27–38. Milan Luglio. https://www.tuttocina.it/Mondo_cinese/108/108_orla.htm.

Orlandi, Romeo. 2006. Qui il piccolo non e' bello. In *Mondo e Mercati, Il Sole 24 Ore*, 12 Sept.

Parenti, Antonio. 2002. *Il WTO*. Bologna: Il Mulino.

Pecorari, Paolo (ed.). 2015. *L'Italia economica. Tempi e fenomeni del cambiamento (1861–2000)*. Padova: Cedam.

Pedretti, Angelo. 1977. La 41° Fiera di Canton e il commercio estero cinese. In *Mondo Cinese* n°18, 99–102. Milan.

Pellegrini, C. G. 1973. *Geografia sociale ed economica della Cina*, Milan: Vita e pensiero pubblicazioni.

Petri, Rolf. 2002. *Storia economica d'Italia. Dalla Grande Guerra al miracolo economico (1918–1963)*. Bologna: Il Mulino.

Picchio, Nicoletta. 2006a. Canton è la porta delle pmi. In *Economia e Impresa, Il Sole 24 Ore*, 16 Sept.

Picchio, Nicoletta. 2006b. Il recupero dell'Italia è già cominciato. *Il Sole 24 Ore*, 14 Sept.

Pollard, Sydney. 2004. *Storia economica del Novecento*. Bologna: Il Mulino. Or. Ed. 1990. *Wealth and poverty. An economic history of the 20th century*. London: Harrap.

Pomeranz, Kenneth. 2000. *The great divergence: China, Europe, and the making of the modern world economy*. Princeton: Princeton University Press.

Porfyriou, Heleni, and Luigi Scaroina, Bing Yu. 2018. Heritage preservation in Italy and China. Legal tools and Institutions. In *China and Italy: routes of culture, valorisation and management*, ed. Porfyriou Heleni, and Bing Yu, 17–31. Rome: Cnr Edizioni.

Postigliola, Michele, and Donatella Strangio. 2017. Il debito pubblico italiano. Una serie storica dal 1861 al 2012. *Storia economica* 20 (1): 313–330.

Rinella, Angelo. 2006. *Cina*, Bologna. Il Mulino.

Romano, Sergio. 1977. *Storia d'Italia dal Risorgimento ai giorni nostri*. Milan: Longanesi.

Rosa, Gabriele. 1868. *La coltura dei bachi nell'Europa*. Brescia: Tipografia Apollono.

SACH. (2017). *A guideline for historic buildings open to the public* (Trial), Wenwubaofa No. 23.

Schmidit-Glintzer, Helwig. 2002. *La Cina contemporanea*. Rome: Carocci.

Schmidt-Glintzer, Helwig. 2005. *Storia della Cina. Dall'impero celeste al boom economico*. Milan: Arnoldo Mondadori Editore.

Secchi, Carlo. 1977. L'Italia e il commercio estero cinese: un aggiornamento. In *Mondo Cinese n.18*, 95–98, Milan.

Sessa, Alfredo. 2006. Dieci scorciatoie per investire bene. In *Mondo e Mercati, Il Sole 24 Ore*, 12 Sept.

Sessa, Alfredo. 2010. *La via della seta parla italiano*. Il Sole24Ore, 11 may. https://st.ilsole24ore.com/art/notizie/2010-05-11/parla-italiano-081000.shtml.

Smith, Adam. 1976. *La ricchezza delle nazioni*. vol. II, Rome: Newton Compton Editori.

Spalletta, Alessandra. 2006. Le pmi la vera locomotiva del Celeste Impero. In *Mondo e Mercati, Il Sole 24 Ore*, 12 Sept.

State Council. (2016). *Guiding opinions on the further strengthening of cultural relics work* (Guofa No. 17).

Stringher, Bonaldo. 1881. *Il biglietto di Stato. Appunti e osservazioni a proposito del disegno di legge sulla estinzione del corso forzoso*. Rome: Eredi Botta.

Teso, Antonio. 1923. *L'Italia e l'Oriente. Studi di politica commerciale* (new edition 2012). Turin: Nabu Press.

Toniolo, Gianni. 1988. *Storia economica dell'Italia liberale 1850–1918*. Bologna: Il Mulino.

Van Der Wee, Herman. 1989. *L'economia mondiale tra crisi e benessere (1945–1980). Una sintesi della storia economica del dopoguerra*. Milan: Editor Ulrico Hoepli (Trad Or. *Prosperity and Upheaval: the World Economy (1945–1980)* Deutscher Taschenbuch Verlag GmbH& Co., Munich 1983–1984).

Vannutelli, C. 1961. Occupazione e salari dal 1861al 1961. In *L'economia italiana dal 1861 al 1961. Studi sul primo censimento dell'Unità d'Italia*, by AA.VV. Milan.

Vinciguerra, Luca. 2006a. Gruppi cinesi in marcia. In *Mondo e Mercati, Il Sole 24 Ore*, 12 Sept.

Vinciguerra, Luca. 2006b. L'Italia rincorre il boom cinese. In *Mondo e Mercati, Il Sole 24 Ore*, 12 Sept.

Vinciguerra, Luca. 2006c. Per l'Italia l'export va meglio. In *Mondo e Mercati, Il Sole 24 Ore*, 12 Sept.

Vinciguerra, Luca. 2006d. Viaggio alle sorgenti del boom. In *Economia e Impresa, Il Sole 24 Ore*, 16 Sept.

Zamagni, Vera. 1976. La dinamica dei salari nel settore industrial. In *L'economia italiana nel periodo fascista*, a cura di Pierluigi Ciocca and Gianni Toniolo, 329–378. Bologna: Il Mulino.

Zamagni, Vera. 1990 (new ed. 1993). *Dalla periferia al centro. La seconda rinascita economica dell'Italia 1861–1981*. Bologna: Il Mulino.

Zamagni, Vera. 2002. Salari e profitti nell'industria italiana tra decollo industriale e anni'30. In *Il lavoro come fattore produttivo e come risorsa nella storia economica italiana*, eds. Sergio Zaninelli e Mario Taccolini, 243–254. Brescia: Vita e Pensiero.

Zamagni, Vera. 2010. *L'industria chimica italiana e l'IMI*. Bologna, Il Mulino: Intesa San Paolo.

Analytical Index

D. Strangio, *Italy-China Trade Relations*, Studies in Economic History,
https://doi.org/10.1007/978-3-030-39084-6

The manufacturer's authorised representative in the EU is Springer Nature Customer Service Centre GmbH, Europaplatz 3, 69115 Heidelberg, Germany. If you have any concerns regarding our products, please contact ProductSafety@springernature.com

Printed and bound by CPI Group (UK) Ltd, Croydon, CR0 4YY
30/09/2026
02225465-0008